# it could be verse

design: Liz Vahlsing, StudioAds, Albany, CA
dingbat art (Big Cheese) and cover/chapter head font (variex)
        from Emigre type, Sacramento, CA, (dingbat art
        designed by Eric Donelan and Bob Aufuldish)


All Inquiries should be addressed to:
 BOAZ
P.O. Box 6582
Albany, CA  94706

distributed by:
Ten Speed Press, Berkeley, CA


Printed in the United States of America


Library of Congress Cataloging-in-publication Data on file
with publisher.

ISBN 0898 157773

# it could be verse

## anybody's guide to Poetry

### joHN timpane

published by:
BOAZ
Albany, CA

distributed by:
Ten Speed Press
Berkeley, CA

# Acknowledgments

In the April 11, 1993, issue of the *San Jose Mercury News*, my article "Poetry in Motion" appeared. That article was the starting point for this book and the starting point for my thanks. So thanks, Sheila Himmel, editor of the Sunday *West* section of the *Mercury News*, for encouraging me and making some fine suggestions. My special thanks to Michael Bugeja, Dan Gottlieb, Ed Ochester, Peter Oresick, Beth Seetch, Vikram Seth, and Lee Upton. Thanks to the twin pillars of Boaz: Tom Southern (for getting after me to write the book) and Liz Vahlsing (for her spectacular originality in design and everything else). Also thanks to Phil Wood and Kirsty Melville of Ten Speed Press, and to Judy Bloch for her insightful, patient, and creative copy-editing. My genuine thanks to thousands of students, writers, and readers who have taught me what poetry can do. I wish I could list all the good teachers in my life, but I will have to roll all of them up into one: Richard Riedel, who got the poems rolling. Thank you, Maria-Christina Keller, for being married to me and making life good, and to Pilar and Conor for letting me be their dad. Thanks to the still, small voice, always with me in everything. And thank you, DR.

# table of contents

# iNtroductioN

## Dear Reader—or DR—

What if I told you there was **all this stuff**, building up for thousands of years but readily available, that could truly make your life better?

Wouldn't you be curious? Just a little?

What if I added that all sorts of people do it, from cowboys to astronauts, from housewives to bank tellers?

Wouldn't you start to wonder just what this was?

What if I said that it's a very well-kept secret in this country—something that makes many people feel dumb, inadequate, something many people are actually **afraid of?**

But that the great thing is, no one needs to fear it?

Wouldn't a short, enthusiastic how-to book on such a thing deserve a place between **How to Get Perfect Revenge Every Time** and **Families: How to Avoid Them?**

And wouldn't you like to **know** what that thing was?

Okay. I'll tell you—but only if you promise not to put down the book for ten more sentences. Deal? Deal.

It's poetry. (Keep reading. You promised.)

Poetry can make life better. Otherwise, why write it? Why read it?

A changed point of view; a sharpened appreciation of life; a mind learning new things about the world, other people's lives, and your own life—DR, if this were a food, the shelves would be sagging with cookbooks on it. If it were a drug, the FDA would have to license it. And, man, would it be expensive.

Here, we'll look at what there is to *like* about poetry. That will mean learning how to read aloud. And how to pay attention. If you want the good stuff poetry has—and there is so much good stuff—you have to **DO IT**.

Some work is involved. Not as much as it takes to lose thirty-five pounds. Not as much as it takes to perfect your golf stroke. About as much as it takes to do origami or refine your wine-tasting skills—maybe a little less.

Here are a few of the features of the book.

 **Anything written in this print is spoken by DR, our Dear Reader. DR voices many of the Person-in-the-Street's doubts and complaints about poetry.**

DR and I have little chats throughout the book. Those chats usually happen at very important places.

Throughout, you will see little icons.

First and most important is this one: **DO** 🏃 **IT**

Meaning: **Time to read the indicated poem aloud.**

The whole point of the book is for you to **DO IT**.

Either you will **DO IT** or you won't.

Life will be better if you **DO IT**. So why not? Play along with an open mind and ready spirit. I promise you pleasures.

Another icon is **I.Q.** 🔥 **meaning Innocent Question.** This marks **a question people feel stupid about asking.** Note: these are usually extremely smart questions.

But for some reason, people—like DR—feel stupid about asking them. I don't know why. Watch DR's questions get smarter and smarter as time goes by.

A third icon is: **BINGO!** 🖐 I use this one when a poem really strikes home, hits the nail on the donkey, sets fire to the goat, rips the clothes off the world and slams its head in the door—that is, when a poem really does what poetry is supposed to do: speak the truth, reveal the world. When I can't help myself, I add an **Uh-huh!** or a **You bet!**

Our last icon appears in our section "Sixty-Six Poets: An Appreciator's Guide": ℙ𝔾ℝ*!!* (Professional Guidance Recommended). This means that you should take a class to get the most out of the poet being discussed. Most poetry, you can just pick up and read, and good things start happening *inmediatamente!* Right away! Good, good things! But with some poets, professional guidance is your best bet. They are miraculous artists— but you need a *Fearless Leader* to show you the way.

All right, friends. Let's take 'em to Missouri.

## Introduction:
# WHY poetry?

If you can't wait to **DO IT**, skip to Chapter One.
At this rate, you'll finish in no time!

**F**or a moment in January 1993, poetry took center on the American stage. Maya Angelou read "On the Pulse of Morning" at the inauguration of President Bill Clinton, becoming the first inaugural poet since James Dickey read "The Strength of Fields" at Jimmy Carter's inauguration in 1977. Not everyone liked Angelou's poem. But like it or hate it, few were indifferent; all were energized, agitated, challenged. For some (for millions, I bet) the inauguration was the first time in years they had heard a poem recited—perhaps the first time ever outside of school. That teaches us an indispensable truth: **when you actually hear and see a poem performed, it can have a tremendous impact**. It can make you think, uplift you, hurt you, baffle you, change your life.

Angelou reminded America about something America had forgotten: the power of poetry to *move*. Why did we forget? Something about poetry has not gotten across. Somebody messed up somewhere. As a result, most of us aren't taking advantage of the full range of pleasures our culture provides.

Some blame the schools; some blame TV, pop music, T. S. Eliot. Let's call the whole thing off. Let's cut through the sociology in the simplest way we know—by getting you to admit you might enjoy poetry.

Like poetry, DR. All by yourself. For your own reasons. Lose this idea that poetry is somehow not for us.

Sure it is for us.

Who else would it be for?

If you can read—if you can hear—you can enjoy poetry. While it can't replace the TV, at least it can't break, and there's always something on.

# American Poetry:
# It's Everywhere—But Where Is It?

One thing is for sure: poetry is flourishing throughout this republic. More Americans are writing it than ever before. Depending on your definition, there may be up to 25,000 professional poets in the United States.

Ground zero for the poetry explosion is the New American Poetry Reading. In Chicago, Boston, New York, Pittsburgh, Santa Fe, San Jose, all over the country, you might go to readings by poets such as Roberto Duran, Jean Emerson, Carolyn Grassi, Phyllis Koestenbaum, Dale Pendell, or Al Young. (Don't worry if you've never heard of them. Once upon a time, William Shakespeare was just a "Hey, you.") No matter who or what you are, there are poets writing about your world.

On airport walls, on public buildings, on the very sidewalks, poetry makes myriad civic appearances. (At the foot of the Statue of Liberty lie an island and a sonnet.) Rapid Transit Poetry is all over the place. Subways in Philadelphia and Boston have slipped poems among the ads for pizzas and weight-loss clinics. The New York City Metropolitan Transit Authority, together with the Poetry Society of America, now has a program, called Poetry in Motion, for straphangers—a captive audience if ever there was one.

There is poetry in the American popular song, the greeting card, the advertisement. Infiniti cars are sold with introspective, inspirational words for the five-figure shopper. A recent Gap ad featured poet Max Blagg reading in a smoky night spot.

Coffeehouses are back, featuring open-mike readings, poetry slams, poetry raves, and poets reading to the sound of jazz. San Francisco's Mission District now hosts a *fin de siècle* version of the 1950s Beat scene. Cincinnati, Los Angeles, and San Diego have their own reading worlds. Coffeehouse poetry is so trendy that it has been satirized on *The Simpsons*.

Even dead poets can pack them in. For the 100th anniversary of the death of Walt Whitman, more than 2,000 people crowded into New York's Cathedral of St. John the Divine to hear Walt's works read by poets such as Galway Kinnell, Gerald Stern, and Sharon Olds.

Lee Upton, poet and teacher at Lafayette College, thinks that the growing popularity of poetry readings says something about the modern condition. "It's wonderful," she says, "to have language in front of us that isn't disposable, isn't trying to get you to buy something." Donald Revell, poet and former editor of the *Denver Quarterly*, agrees: "After the trickle-down emptiness of the 1980s, people perhaps wanted some alternative, some substance."

Imagine millions of schoolkids encouraged to try rhyme, haiku, or free verse; teenagers with their journals; people turning to poetry to help them suffer through or recover from tragedy; the joyous or perplexed who grab pen and paper; the teachers who use poetry to teach medicine, science, engineering, and ethics; the senators, presidents, representatives, and spokespeople who quote poetry to make a point they can make in no other way; and, atop the pop heap, rap.

Hellishly repetitious most of the time, rap has its subtleties. The best rappers, such as the Digable Planets in "Rebirth of Slick," can take a line such as "I'm cool like dat," eight times different ways and say eight different things; then they'll throw in "I'm chill like dat" and "I'm black like dat," do the same with them, and suddenly you have twenty-four statements, all different, all interrelated. Chauvinist, racist, violent, notorious for exploiting both performers and audience, rap can make you pay attention and deliver you to the truth. Now in its second decade, rap may be on its way out, but it speaks the street, has got a good beat, and counts as poetry, like it or not.

Americans are using poetry in many ways. They use it in teaching—and not just in English class. Anthony Petrosky, poet and professor at the Pittsburgh University School of Education, says that poetry helps make students better thinkers. "Poetry can be an excellent means of teaching people to use details and particulars," he says. "It makes them better observers."

They've taught engineering at MIT and Cal Tech with poetry. Robert Coles, professor of psychology at Harvard University, has used poems to teach students the art of medicine. Why poems? Coles writes that patients and doctors alike "long for someone's help in making sense of it all." Poems offer "the epiphanies doctors and patients alike crave." A good doctor needs to know how a dying patient feels. To learn, read just two lines from L. E. Sissman's poem "A Death Place":

> Very few people know where they will die,
> But I do: in a brick-faced hospital

Sissman, who died of cancer, knew what he was writing about.

One place poetry directly benefits people is in therapy. Dan Gottlieb, a psychologist and the host of *Voices in the Family* on National Public Radio, uses poetry in healing. "Many of my guest therapists use poems. I use them all the time," he says. One of his callers, an exhausted, distraught woman trying to care for a schizophrenic family member, declared that none of her love and work could get a response. Gottlieb responded with Richard Wilbur's poem "The Writer." The last three lines spoke to and for her:

> It is always a matter, my darling,
> Of life or death, as I had forgotten. I wish
> What I wished you before, but harder.

"It's one of my favorites," Gottlieb says, "and I've used it in many settings. A poem I find myself using a lot lately is the Maya Angelou poem. Three lines in particular seem to hit a chord with many of the people I work with:

> History, despite its wrenching pain,
> Cannot be unlived, but if faced
> With courage, need not be lived again.

That's talking about nations, and it's talking about people."

Because it is so hard to speak of the human heart directly, the therapist, like the poet, must turn to metaphors. "What I do for a living is to speak to people's hearts," Gottlieb says. "Poets do that courageously and directly. There lies a deep healing power in the way metaphors communicate. My patients speak in metaphors. Their dreams are metaphors. That's why poetry speaks directly to them, consciously and unconsciously." And poetry lets us know we do not suffer by ourselves. "Reading poems can make people feel less alone with their problems," Gottlieb says, "You know somebody else in the past has been where you are."

Some use poems to be better at business. Dana Gioia, once an executive with General Foods and now a full-time poet and critic, is mindful of belonging to a line of American business people who were also poets. (Wallace Stevens was an executive for Hartford Accident and Indemnity, and T. S. Eliot was a foreign-exchange correspondent for Lloyd's Bank.) In Gioia's poem "The Man in the Open Doorway," a businessman may drive back to the office to work late

> And, thinking of the day's success,
> Trace his steps once more,
>
> Then pause in a darkened stairway
> Until the sounds of his steps have ceased
> And stroke the wall as if it were
> Some attendant beast.

Here's the paradox: Poetry is everywhere—but where is poetry? Not on TV. Not on radio. If poetry has exploded, the explosion has been pretty quiet. Perhaps other things are performing the role poetry once played. Peter Oresick, assistant director and promotion and marketing manager for the University of Pittsburgh Press, says that "poetry's social role has been usurped by other media—especially the popular song, which has done more to take away from the role of poetry than anything else." Once it was Bob Dylan, Joni Mitchell, the Beatles; today, it might be the Indigo Girls, U2, Ice-T. Go out on any schoolyard and be amazed as seven-year-olds recite the latest rap song word for word, rhythm for rhythm.

Poetry has long held an uneasy place in our culture. Many are the reasons. The poet Gerald Stern says, "It may be a throwback to the Puritan ethic: people are uncomfortable with anything that doesn't seem to have an immediate use." This is partly the fault of the poets. The first half of this century saw the rise of austere, dif-

7

ficult poets such as T. S. Eliot and Ezra Pound. And some poets continue to write intellectual, baffling poetry that is assured of a very small audience. But not all poets write this way. Poet Vikram Seth says, "Really, it strikes me as unfair of so many professional poets to insist on being so difficult."

Children and adolescents are deeply drawn to poetry. But then something terrible happens. Michael J. Bugeja, poet and professor at the E. W. Scripps School of Journalism, surveyed his students to determine the reasons they had stopped liking poetry. One-third of them reported giving up when teachers criticized their interpretations.

"As teachers," Bugeja says, "we have to ask ourselves what in heck we're doing when we present a poem, the student expresses some joy in the poem, and is told, 'You're wrong! You get an F!'"

Which of the following false truisms did you learn in school?

- ⬧ All poetry rhymes.
- No poetry rhymes anymore.
- ⬧ Poetry is primarily a way to express yourself.
- No: Poetry speaks for all humanity.
- ⬧ Poetry is a great repository of emotions.
- No: Ideas, yeah, that's it, ideas.
- ⬧ Well, OK then, stories.
- No, no: It's images, whatever they are.

All are true, all are garbage. Worst of all is the idea that poetry is something that should be analyzed. Too often the result is that, in Oresick's words, "poetry is the one art form that consistently makes people feel stupid."

There's a national movement to change how poetry is taught. Gioia calls on high school and college teachers to "spend less time on analysis and more on performance." Poems should be "memorized, recited, and performed," he writes, to get back to the sheer "sensual excitement of speaking and hearing the words of the poem." Bugeja says, "I'd encourage teachers, please, to put more focus on appreciating poetry and less on explicating and interpreting it."

Perhaps the next generation of schoolchildren will learn that poetry can, in Oresick's words, "make you smile as much as any TV can."

## A Bowl of Reasons

There are four reasons for you to take up poetry.

**Pleasure**. Poetry can give you intense pleasures you can't get anywhere else. When, in his poem "Among School Children," W. B. Yeats writes

> O chestnut tree, great-rooted blossomer,
> Are you the leaf, the blossom or the bole?
> O body swayed to music, O brightening glance,
> How can we know the dancer from the dance?

it's supposed to give you pleasure. Poetry can truly intoxicate. Emily Dickinson once wrote, "If I feel physically as if the top of my head were taken off, I know that this is poetry."

Not an especially dainty thing for our Emily to say!

There's more to pleasure than self-pleasure. Pleasure also leads to

**Truth**. A popular prejudice holds that poetry is somehow not "in touch" with the world. Bunk.

Many folks read poetry to learn the truth about people's lives. Donald Revell says, "Poetry lets you know what you're doing, who you are. It's a form of self-knowledge, a form of mental health."

Open an anthology such as *Working Classics* (see page 88) and you will find in condensed form the essence of hundreds of lives, as in Ed Ochester's poem "The Miners at Revloc":

> Coal has entered their skin.
> A fine black salt drifts
> back into their meals.
> Every day the mills are fed
> tiny wafers of their flesh.

Now we have learned something about the lives of mine workers.

When life is joyful, poetry is there to say it, as in William Blake's "Infant Joy":

"I have no name,
I am but two days old."
What shall I call thee?
"I happy am,
Joy is my name."
Sweet joy befall thee!

Joy is the truth sometimes. Now, some kinds of truth are to be learned for their own sake, and others are there to be used. That brings us to the idea that

**Poetry can help you.** It's a possibility. Poetry may help you see your own life more clearly, compare your outlook to that of other people. Vikram Seth is impressed by the way in which people of many cultures turn to poetry for comfort. "At the time of the Cultural Revolution, and again after Tiananmen Square, the Chinese turned to their famous old poets for solace," Seth says. "You find this in Russia, and also in India. Solace is one of the major benefits poetry can give its readers."

People have become friends, formed communities, decided to part, act, procreate, all on the basis of what they have found in poems. Writing a poem, after all, is an active thing—as reading it should be. We think of poetry as passive and inert, when in fact it is anchored in the world and calls us to anchor there too. That is why

**Reading poetry is both intensely personal and the ultimate unselfish act.** It starts as something you do for yourself—an alternative in the pleasure-round of American culture. Stay with it and you will find that poetry connects you to the world and the people in it.

**Reading poetry
is a way of
paying attention.**

And paying attention is a good thing to do.

It's a way of being involved, of bridging your own aspirations to those of all humanity.

That could make yours a fuller life—and all for less than $30. May you read a poem here and there. May it give you pleasure, truth, help, a reason to say, along with Elizabeth Socolow, "I am alive **/** and kick my heels at the stars."

# Chapter One:
# reading aLoud

Welcome to the audience participation segment of this book.

Repeat after me:

 **Poetry is meant to be read aloud.**

Excuse me.

The request was to repeat the line.

Speak it aloud:

 **Poetry is meant to be read aloud.**

Hmmm. We're going to have to stand up and say the words in a distinct, positive voice. If for any reason you can't make it to your feet, make up for it in volume. This is an important sentence you are about to speak. Here's your first **DO IT**, my friend.

 **Poetry is meant to be read aloud.**

We're serious.

Not reading a poem aloud is like not living in your house after you've built it. Why would you do that to a poem? Just leave it sitting there, silent, a bunch of marks on the page? When all it wants to do is leap out of your throat in all the fun and surprise and pleasure it can pack?

Let's be nice to poems—and, more importantly, to ourselves—and read aloud.

**All right**, not always. Not in the shower, because it will ruin the book. Not in church, because it will ruin your reputation. Not, or at least not always, on the train—check to see whether the people next to you are receptive (or asleep).

But everywhere else, of course. In the library? *Como no*? (Softly.) In the car? As long as you're not driving. In the living room? Well, yes—what, is it a sin to turn off the tube and actually *do* something?

**Isn't it sort of silly to read stuff aloud?**

**Answer**: It's very silly, it misses the whole point, not to. Poems, DR, are made of words, with all their sounds and rhythms. Inserting them directly into your grey matter—without giving them voice—is a big mistake. It's like planting your new rose bush *all the way* in the ground.

Major pleasure loss. Understanding loss. Rose loss. Grey matter loss.

Reading poems silently can actually make you more stupid. *Everyone's* unhappy.

Therefore the mantra of this book is **DO IT**. The "**IT**" is reading aloud. As I said, every time you see this icon—

—you actually read the ensuing passage aloud. With your voice. So you can hear it.

Once again, either you'll **DO IT** or you won't.

If you don't, well, you'll still be good. But why not get better?

**I.Q.** 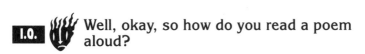 **Well, okay, so how do you read a poem aloud?**

**Thank You** for asking. The Best of All Possible Answers is: *Any Way You Want To.*

After all—why let some strange fellow tell you what to do? (Have you seen my haircut? My taste in clothes? I ask you, why trust me?)

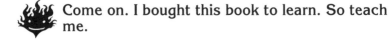 **Come on. I bought this book to learn. So teach me.**

**You bet.** Let's read a poem first and then discuss technique. Here is a marvelous poem for reading aloud: Helen Chasin's "The Word *Plum*."

Read it through. Silently first. We'll wait. Get a preliminary grip on it.

All right. On yer feet, troops. Read clearly, positively, and happily. Let's actually have fun. Get into the sounds; ham it up (no one will know). You're one of thousands doing this very thing right now. (Hint: Pause a little at the ends of the lines, and a little more when there is white space between groups of lines.) **DO IT**

The word *plum* is delicious

pout and push, luxury of
self-love, and savoring murmur

full in the mouth and falling
like fruit

taut skin
pierced, bitten, provoked into
juice, and tart flesh

question
and reply, lip and tongue
of pleasure.

Yum. Read it aloud again, biting into the words. **DO IT** Funny thing about this poem: some people like it for celebrating the fun word *plum*; some like it for evoking the excellent moment you bite into a plum; others suspect this is not altogether an innocent poem. I have no idea what any of them are talking about.

**I.Q. Well, I did it, but I didn't really know what I was doing. It didn't rhyme. What do the white spaces mean? And the punctuation is, well, nonstandard. I'm beginning to feel stupid.**

Fend it off, DR!

These questions mean *you're smart*—you've already started noticing things!

And poetry is a way of paying attention.

Let's look at your questions:

 **Question One: Why Didn't the Thing Rhyme?**

**Answer**: Because it didn't. Much of the greatest poetry in the universe doesn't. Much also does. This poem happens not to. Hang in there.

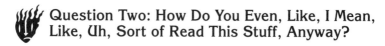 Question Two: How Do You Even, Like, I Mean, Like, Uh, Sort of Read This Stuff, Anyway?

**Suggestions, or, For Those Who Prefer Them, Commandments:**

🏃 **First read the poem silently, to get a feeling for it.**

🦶 **Now prepare to read aloud. Assume that the speaker of the poem is speaking in a conversational way. That person has something important and surprising to tell you.**

So how do people speak who have important, surprising things to tell you? NOT in a monotone. NOT slurring their words. In most North American mouths, "Shall I compare thee to a summer's day?" can degrade into "Shly cmparr theetoass ummersday" with no question mark—it's a horrible travesty.

☞ **Speak distinctvely and positively, with a little push behind the words.**

Avoid the way most North Americans speak, in a nasal, slurred monotone. Instead:

☞ **Use your chest and throat. Speak expressively.**

☞ *Look for surprises and gently emphasize them.*

On the average, each line of poetry contains at least one surprise word. Look at

The word *plum* is delicious

Gently humorous, no? Playful, no? The word *delicious* is delicious. And the statement is that a *word* is delicious. Sure, plums are delicious, but words? *Two whole surprises in five words! Continue if you*

**14**

*dare!* When you read that line—be positive now, and speak distinctly—you're going to emphasize *delicious* as well as *plum.*

How can you not?

 **DO IT** The word PLUM is deLIcious

Mmmm mmm.

☞ *Use slight pauses as emphasis.*

Ever-so-slight pauses. Let's call them "beats," and, if they're small, "bips." A bip is half of a beat. (Such an intellectual book.) A natural beat comes after *plum*—and a bip could come just before *delicious*, because that's the surprise word.

The word *plum* [beat] is [bip] deLIcious      **DO IT**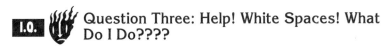

Hey hey.

**I.O.**  Question Three: Help! White Spaces! What Do I Do????

All right, all right, all right.

Where there are words, read the words. Where there are no words, wait a bit until more words come.

 I want a rule.

Okay, have a rule:

☞ **Treat white space as time.** Pause gently at the end of lines—unless it's awkward. Add pauses if the poem skips lines or if lines are indented.

**I.O.** How long is an end-of-line pause?

Sometimes a beat, sometimes a bip. Let the sense of the poem guide you.

One other thing about line endings:

☞ **At the end of lines that don't end in punctuation marks, lift your tone of voice just a little.** Give a sense of expectancy, of being pulled into the next line.

Don't overdo it. Otherwise, a certain Valley Girl syndrome may set in:

The word *plum* is delicious?

pout and push? luxury of?
self-love? and savoring murmur?

full in the mouth and falling?

I hope somebody's laughing because I am close to tears. At line endings without punctuation, just give your voice a tiny upswing of expectancy.

And a general rule:

☞ **No need to rush.** Could be a popular bumper sticker, couldn't it? **No Need To Rush.** This wait-a-bit rule helps surprises pop out:

> The word *plum* is delicious [beat]
> pout and push, luxury of [bip]
> self-love

**I get it.** You put a beat after *delicious* because the first line is more of a complete statement. The second line sort of hangs there incomplete, so it gets a bip. So that second line is a good place to use my little expectant tone?

You bet! Poets use line spacings, white spaces, and indentations to direct your attention, get you to emphasize different things—to guide the way you read the poem. Look at this one, by our mal-typewriting friend, e. e. cummings:

Buffalo Bill's
defunct
    who used to
    ride a watersmooth-silver
                stallion
and break onetwothreefourfive pigeonsjustlikethat
                              Jesus
he was a handsome man
                and what i want to know is
how do you like your blueeyed boy
Mister Death

When words run together, read them fast. When Buffalo Bill is shooting at them clay pigeons, it's truly onetwothreefourfive. Load the last lines, though, with pauses—they are, after all, pretty heavy. Really helps that poem live, doesn't it? Death came to Buffalo Bill Cody, as it will to those of us who can nary lasso a cayuse.

Let's review our Nine Commandments for Reading Aloud:

☞ **First** read the poem **silently**, to get a feeling for it.

☞ **Now** prepare to **read aloud**. Assume that the speaker of the poem is speaking in a conversational way. That person has something important and surprising to tell you.

☞ Speak distinctly and positively, **with a little push behind the words**.

☞ Avoid the way most North Americans speak—in a nasal, slurred monotone. Use your chest and throat. Speak expressively.

☞ **Look for surprises** and gently emphasize them.

☞ Use slight **pauses** as **emphasis**.

☞ Treat **white space as time**. Pause gently at the end of lines—unless it's awkward. Add pauses if the poem skips lines or if lines are indented.

☞ At the end of lines that don't end in punctuation marks, **lift your tone of voice** just a little. Give a sense of expectancy, of being pulled into the next line.

☞ **No need to rush**.

Some people like to pencil-mark the words they are going to emphasize and the places they are going to pause. If this strikes you as anal, like labeling every egg in the fridge, well, don't do it. If it helps, do it. Try reading the poem again, paying attention to the surprises, the rhythms, the jokes, the whole package.

 We'll wait.

*Fun* is the subject, although there are other subjects in there, too (snicker, wink wink, nudge nudge). But that's for you to think about.

# The Rhyme and Rhythm to Rhyme and Rhythm

 How about some rhyming poetry to practice on?

Okay. Here's a stanza from "I Knew a Woman" by Theodore Roethke.

I knew a woman, lovely in her bones,
When small birds sighed, she would sigh back at them;
Ah, when she moved, she moved more ways than one:
The shapes a bright container can contain!
Of her choice virtues only gods should speak,
Or English poets who grew up on Greek
(I'd have them sing in chorus, cheek to cheek).

You can still use all our rules, but now there is one more, to make Ten Commandments:

☞ **In poems with meter and rhyme, read with rhythm, but don't get sing-songy**.

You know. Sing-songy. The nasal fourth-grade no-brain idiot/machine/slobbermouth yadda-yadda monotone of "I SHOT an ARrowin TO the YARE, it FELL to EARTH, i KNOW NOT WHERE."

Will someone please shoot us? Now. End this horrible life.

Don't do this to a beautiful poem. Give each word its due. Poetry is a way of paying attention. So don't read it

i KNEW a WOOman LOVEly IN her BONES

which should be punishable by life imprisonment without parole. Let the rhythm be more conversational, bump up against the surprises and pauses in the sentence.

i KNEW a WOman [beat] LOVEly [bip] in her BONES

and speak the word *lovely* as though you meant it—because you do. The truth (in this poem) is, **dat woman wuz lovely**. The speaker is leaning across the table and **informing** you.

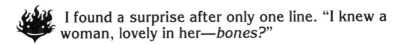 I found a surprise after only one line. "I knew a woman, lovely in her—*bones?*"

Good one, DR. Lots of people are lovely in lots of, um, areas. This woman evidently was lovely through and through. Find this poem (in many good anthologies of American poetry; see pages 86-88) and read the rest of it. By the end, you'll get the feeling you know this woman—and the speaker.

## Meter Versus Rhythm Versus You

Time to exercise our newfound skills. Here is a poem by Philip Larkin.

Peruse, read, repeat.  **DO** **IT**

### The Trees

The trees are coming into leaf
Like something almost being said;
The recent buds relax and spread,
Their greenness is a kind of grief.

Is it that they are born again
And we grow old? No, they die too.
Their yearly trick of looking new
Is written down in rings of grain.

Yet still the unresting castles thresh
In fullgrown thickness every May.
Last year is dead, they seem to say,
Begin afresh, afresh, afresh.

You gotta have rhythm. Rhythm is what isn't regular.
Rhythm is the natural set of stresses in each line, the way you would stress those stresses if you were a human being.
Which you are.

Sure, the poem starts out with a pretty regular lilt—

The TREES are COMing INto LEAF
Like SOMEthing ALmost BEing SAID

—but!! resist the temptation to be sing-songy. Try some pauses to derail the Brainless Train:

The trees [here] are coming [or here] into [or here] leaf

Or you could read that first line

The TREES are COMing into [beat] LEAF

 We'll wait.
Nice.
Now would anyone with more than the intelligence of a broccoli read the lines this way?:

Is IT that THEY are BORN aGAIN
And WE grow OLD? No, THEY die TOO.

An insult to broccoli. As before, try to let the rhythm be more conversational, bump up against the surprises and pauses in the sentence:

IS it that THEY are [beat] BORN aGAIN
And WE GROW OLD? NO, [beat] THEY DIE TOO.

 Eleven stresses in two lines.

**Yep.** That second line is slowwww, DR—see all those *o* sounds slowing down the old line?

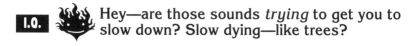 Hey—are those sounds *trying* to get you to slow down? Slow dying—like trees?

Maybe we should split the advance on this book! I hope you enjoy this poem. It's full of awe at the trees, at their energy each spring. There's sadness in there too. But, DR, that last line— "Begin afresh, afresh, afresh"—is fun to read, and it comes down on the splendid side of spring.

I *tricked* you, DR!

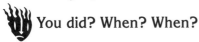 **You did? When? When?**

I used that last poem to teach you the difference between

**METER**

(which always stays the same)

and

**RHYTHM**

(which is different from line to line).

The **meter** of the Larkin poem is this:

duh DAH duh DAH duh DAH duh DAH

A single *duh DAH*, or short-long, is called an *iamb*. (Mysterious ancient Greek words!) There are four *duh DAH*s in this meter, making it iambic tetrameter (*tetrameter* means "a measure of four," so *iambic tetrameter* means "a measure of four iambs"). The dictionary stresses of the words in the first line,

The TREES are COMing INto LEAF

go, or pretty nearly,

duh DAH duh DAH duh DAH duh DAH

if you let them. That means that its **rhythm** (the dictionary stresses the words) and its **meter** are pretty much the same:

The TREES are COMing INto LEAF

(meter)    duh DAH duh DAH duh DAH duh DAH

(rhythm)   duh DAH duh DAH duh DAH duh DAH

**But it won't stay like that.** Meter is just an imaginary pattern; you're not supposed to let it straightjacket you. A good poet chooses a meter and, at least initially, adheres closely to it, as Larkin does. But after a few lines everybody gets completely bored, so you start getting lines like

IS it that THEY are BORN aGAIN
(meter)     duh DAH duh DAH duh DAH duh DAH
(rhythm)  DAH duh duh DAH duh DAH duh DAH

and after a while, when we're really getting crazy,

Yet STILL the unRESTing CASTles THRESH
(meter)    duh DAH duh DAH duh DAH duh DAH
(rhythm)  duh DAH duh duh DAH duh DAH duh DAH

 **So the meter is just something in your head? Something abstract? And the rhythm is what you actually read? Not the meter?**

You're cooking with natural gas now, DR. The meter is something the poet sets up in your head, much as a drummer might rap out an intro to a song, to give you the time signature.

That's right. The difference between meter and rhythm is the difference between the beat of a song and what's actually played over the beat.

Let's take the nursery rhyme "Bah Bah, Black Sheep." Rap out the beat on your lap (1-2-3-4) while singing it. I dare you. For the sake of your social reputation, do this while alone, or in a group of people who know you well. We'll wait. When you sing

Baa baa black sheep,
have you any wool?
Yes sir, yes sir,
three bags full.

the beat is

1 2 3 4
1 2 3 4
1 2 3 4
1 2 3 4

But you're not singing one syllable to one beat in every line, are you? If you did, you'd sound like a gorilla on Valium:

> Bah bah black sheep
> have you aaaa neee . . . uh, wool?

No. You're singing

> Baa baa black sheep,
> have you any wool?

The first line has one syllable to one beat—but not the second! See how the rhythm is different—it's got to be—from the beat. The beat (the meter) stays the same always—you always know it's there, metronome-regular—but the rhythm is the living, breathing variation from line to line.

Now you're on your own.

Below is a sonnet by Howard Nemerov. It's written in **iambic pentameter**.

 **Oh, God—we learned that in school. It's five of those iambs, right?**

**You bet!** Your mission is to read this to yourself, decide how to read it, look up the word *embowering*, and then read the poem aloud.

We'll wait. ███████████████████ **DO** 🏃 **IT**

### Two Girls

I saw again in a dream the other night
Something I saw in daylight years ago,
A path in the rainy woods, a shaft of light,
And two girls walking together through shadow,
Through dazzle, till I lost them on their way
In gloom embowering beyond the glade.
The bright oblivion that belongs to day

Covered their steps, nothing of them remained,
Until the darkness brought them forth again
To the rainy glitter and the silver light,
The ancient leaves that had not fallen then.
Two girls, going forever out of sight,
Talking of lovers, maybe, and of love:
Not that blind life they'd be the mothers of.

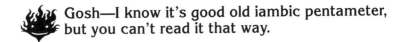 **Gosh—I know it's good old iambic pentameter,
but you can't read it that way.**

Sure can't. If you do, the first line will come out

I SAW aGAIN in A dream THE oTHER . . . night?

Nonsensicalness! Say it as you would say it:

       I SAW aGAIN in a DREAM the OTHer NIGHT
(meter)   duh DAH duh DAH duh DAH duh DAH duh DAH
(rhythm) duh DAH duh DAH duh duh DAH duh DAH duh DAH.

**Or how about**

     And TWO GIRLS WALKing toGETHer through SHADow
(meter)   duh DAH duh DAH duh DAH duh DAH duh DAH
(rhythm) duh DAH DAH DAH duh duh DAH duh duh DAH duh.

The whole poem is like that. It speaks conversationally over the
meter.

 **Yeah—but you can always hear the meter in the
background.**

**You bet!**

# Music, Maestro

Nemerov knew what he was doing. Looking closely at his poem can teach us something about rhyme. Look at the end words, DR. What do you see?

 Let's see . . . *night* rhymes with *light.*

That's called **exact rhyme**, the kind that is most familiar. Keep going.

 Then there is *ago* with *shadow.* That's weird.

Why? It rhymes, doesn't it?

 Yes, but . . . well . . . he rhymed a stressed syllable (aGO) with an unstressed one (SHAdow). Can you do that?

Perfectly legal. No thunderbolts from the sky. Happens all the time.

 Then there is *way* with *glade.*

He's just rhyming the long *a* sound. Call it **vowel rhyme**.

 And *remained* with *again*, which doesn't really rhyme.

Not exactly, no. But it *is* what they call a **slant rhyme**, a little to the side of exact. Also, there's the *AIN* in both words—providing us with **sight rhyme.**

 So there's more to rhyme than I thought.

Read these lines from Dylan Thomas's "And Death Shall Have No Dominion" and find the rhymes.

When their bones are picked clean and the clean bones gone,
They shall have stars at elbow and foot;
Though they go mad they shall be sane,
Though they sink through the sea they shall rise again;
Though lovers be lost love shall not;
And death shall have no dominion.

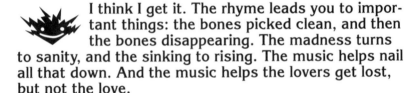

**Whew! That first line has *bones*, which sort of rhymes with *clean*, which sort of rhymes with *gone*, which sort of rhymes with *sane*. You have *foot* rhyming with *not* . . . it really stretches your ears.**

Stretch away, DR. Rhyme is the repetition of sounds, and it happens all over the place—not just at the ends of lines. (When it happens in the middle of lines, as it does in Thomas's poem, we call it **internal rhyme.**) There are many shades of it. Poets use these shadings to reinforce (or to create!) the meanings of the lines.

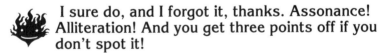

**I think I get it. The rhyme leads you to important things: the bones picked clean, and then the bones disappearing. The madness turns to sanity, and the sinking to rising. The music helps nail all that down. And the music helps the lovers get lost, but not the love.**

**Music**—let's use that word. Remember all you learned in school about how poetry uses sound?

**I sure do, and I forgot it, thanks. Assonance! Alliteration! And you get three points off if you don't spot it!**

We have a glossary somewhere in this book with words like that in it. Some people find them useful.

Our point here, DR, is that poetry is full of **music**—orchestrated sounds that help you feel a certain way.

**Poets use sounds to make you feel the reality of something!**

Some music is just luscious, gorgeous, flowing, sweet, ravishing. Alfred, Lord Tennyson, was good for that:

Now sleeps the crimson petal, now the white;
Nor waves the cypress in the palace walk;
Nor winks the gold fin in the porphyry font:
The fire-fly wakens: waken thou with me.
                        ("Now Sleeps the Crimson Petal")

There is liquid, whispery loveliness in those lines. Read the last two lines aloud, getting your tongue and lips lightly into the words:

Nor winks the gold fin in the porphyry font:
The fire-fly wakens: waken thou with me.

So what do you hear?

 **A lot of *F*s and *W*s. A lot of *I*s and *O*s. You almost have to whisper these lines.**

When poets want you to feel soft, relaxed feelings, as Tennyson did, they can use music like that—gentle and murmuring. When they want to uplift, poets can use another kind:

The world is charged with the grandeur of God.

That's Gerard Manley Hopkins, and all those *r*s and *g*s give muscle to this line from "God's Grandeur." When poets want to give a feeling of giddy happiness, music helps them do that:

Everyone suddenly burst out singing;
And I was filled with such delight
As prisoned birds must find in freedom,
Winging wildly across the white
Orchards and dark-green fields; on — on — and out of sight.
                        ("Everyone Sang")

Siegfried Sassoon wrote that. Say "Winging wildly across the white" five times fast!

 **It's a wild line.**

**Uh-huh!**

What I want you to know, DR, is that all poems *have* music. Like rhythm, music is *part* of the words, but it's *more than* the words, too.

Sometimes you can get meaning from *sound* even when you don't know what the *words* mean. Here's a case in point: in the original Hebrew, some passages from the Book of Isaiah.

 **You're not going to make me read *them* aloud, are you? I don't even know Hebrew!**

Me too, neither. I want you to read the words and guess, by their sound alone, what the subject is. Words—the final frontier! Read that thing!

> boqeq . . . bolqah . . . hiboq tiboq ha'arets
>   hiboz tiboz . . .
> 'abelah nabela ha'arets
>   'umlalah nabelah tebel.
>
> ro'ah hitro'e'ah ha'arets
>   por hitporerah 'arets
> mot hitmotetah 'arets
>   no'a tanu'a 'arets.

Now. Considering the sheer *sounds* in this passage, would you say it's about

**a**) sleep
**b**) shepherds
**c**) earthquakes
**d**) wine

If you said "c) earthquakes," you probably read ahead. Does this passage not rumble and shake? Luis Alonso Shökel, a biblical scholar, says that an English equivalent might be "the earth shivers and staggers, stumbles and tumbles, quivers and quavers and quakes, jars and jerks and jolts." The sounds in themselves get the quake across.

Music can be beautiful, happy, powerful—or, when ugly is appropriate, ugly.

 **Excuse me?**

Not all music is sweet, you know. Nor is all poetry. Poets use sounds to make you feel the reality of something. Here is a splendid example of truly ugly music, by the Irish poet Seamus Heaney, from a poem called "Death of a Naturalist." A little boy, who thinks he wants to be a scientist when he grows up, discovers a frog pond and what it's really like. Read this aloud, and see if you're not, um, riveted. **DO IT**

> Then one hot day when fields were rank
> With cowdung in the grass the angry frogs
> Invaded the flax-dam; I ducked through hedges
> To a coarse croaking that I had not heard
> Before. The air was thick with a bass chorus.
> Right down the dam gross-bellied frogs were cocked
> On sods; their loose necks pulsed like sails. Some hopped:
> The slap and plop were obscene threats. Some sat
> Poised like mud grenades, their blunt heads farting.
> I sickened, turned, and ran. The great slime kings
> Were gathered there for vengeance and I knew
> That if I dipped my hand the spawn would clutch it.

Yecchh! One of the few poems that make you want to scrub your hands after reading. But a feast of noise. How about those lines

> Right down the dam gross-bellied frogs were cocked
> On sods; their loose necks pulsed like sails. Some hopped:
> The slap and plop were obscene threats. Some sat
> Poised like mud grenades, their blunt heads farting.

Practice really getting into those consonants—the *r*s; the *g*s; the fat, warty *p*s. **DO IT** We'll wait.

And now, everyone together, for the really explosive lines. Lay into them with your mouth, lips, and jaw. Drawl the horrible sounds roundly. **DO IT**

> The slap and plop were obscene threats. Some sat
> Poised like mud grenades, their blunt heads farting.

Whew. You can't say the poem is pleasant—but it's vivid. You've had an experience. And that last line is a mini-horror movie of the mind.

And, surprise, DR. Did you notice what the meter of the poem was?

 **Uh, no. Let me go back and read it aloud.**

**DO IT** We'll wait.

 **It's good old iambic pentameter—only he plays around with it!**

Yep. Old Seamus likes to play with his meters—but "Death of a Naturalist" is in very good, very old iambic pentameter.

## Practice Makes More Practice

You're the star of this book. Practice reading aloud. Almost any poem in the book is good practice. Time to get those reading muscles in shape; further guidance is coming in the next chapter. And **DO**  **IT** , baby.

**I.O.**  **I'm not going to turn into an, an . . . an *intellectual*, am I?**

Hey, we like you as you are.

Our whole thing is this: Poetry is about life.

It's about how people live, what they see, what happens to them, and how they feel about it.

Poetry can teach you to love language—those crazy barks that come out of the human face. Language is experience, too, you know.

 **So the more I pay attention, the more good things I'll get out . . .**

Of poetry and life both. People use poetry to explore. Surprises happen, some happy, some not. Some confusing. Sure, it can be intense—but that's part of the pleasure. When you read poetry or write it, the point is: What's happening now? and now? and now?

Poetry, DR, is a way of paying attention.

Pay it, baby.

# Chapter Two:
# tHe poetry Workout

Got your sweats on?
Done your stretches?
Great. Stop immediately if you feel any pain.

**Ground rules**:

**1**. Below you will encounter a very friendly course of poems to read. Follow our Ten Commandments for Reading Aloud (page 17 and 18). Disregard any rule that makes you crazy.

**2**. Read the poem aloud, taking your time, as if the words were yours and you meant every one of them.

**3**. Repeat step 2.

**4**. Enjoy the poem in any way you wish. You do not have to *interpret* the poem—just look for reasons to *like* it.

## Day One: Breaking a Sweat

Let's begin with poems of one line. Because these tend to go by quickly, we must read slowly, with care. Here is a poem titled "Elegy" by the American poet W. S. Merwin. (An *elegy*, by the way, is a song or poem of lamentation or sorrow.)

Who would I show it to

 **Poor person has a song or poem of sorrow and no one to show it to.**

A true song of sorrow. Read it aloud again.

 **That wasn't so bad. In fact, it was nice.**

Now that we've worked up a sweat, I think we're ready to move up to Two Lines. Read the following through to yourself, to get the words right. Then read the poem aloud. Consider what it's saying. Let it resonate. Rinse and repeat.

I hate and yet I love. Perhaps you ask, "How?"
Don't know — but I feel it happening and am tormented.


Tell me you need to be an English major, or any major, to
appreciate that poem.  Read it aloud again.  [ DO ]
Perhaps you have been in this situation or know someone who
has.  Did you sympathize?  Did you suffer?  Are you suffering
now?  If so, take this poem as your own.

If you enjoy that poem even a little, then you like poetry—and
Latin poetry at that, for this was written by Gaius Valerius
Catullus, a Roman poet of the first century B.C. Here you started
this book as a normal person, and you're ending up a Latin scholar.
It's unbelievable.  Lest the humor of the situation overwhelm us,
read the poem aloud once more.

I think we're ready to scale the Mountain of Three Lines.
These particular three lines are from "Prayers and Sayings of the
Mad Farmer" by a wonderful poet, Wendell Berry.

Let me wake in the night
and hear it raining
and go back to sleep.

Me too.

Me too.

Here. Have a song from the Mandan and Hidatsa Indians.

You did it
therefore
you wept.


In the words of Jay Leno, "About says it all, don't it?"  Read once
again aloud: "You did it [beat] therefore [beat] you wept."  See
how important the pauses can be? You may even have a wry smile
at this point.  You did it, therefore you smile.

You're improving with every poem.

I think we're about ready for a **metaphor**—hey, wait a minute. You're running off the field and heading straight for the showers!

 I'm history. Metaphors are where all the trouble began. They're hard. I got to hate them in school. It's not always clear what's a metaphor and what it's a metaphor for. And I never know what a metaphor is supposed to *mean*.

Take a deep breath, DR. Who says you have to *know*? I don't. There will be no quiz here.

**I.Q.**  Can I ask what a metaphor is again?

We—you, I, everybody—make metaphors when we compare thing A to thing B without saying so. For example, this is a metaphor:

You are a snake in the grass.

Now compare that with this, which is an example of a **simile**:

You are like a snake in the grass.

 The first one packs more of a punch. It's a bigger insult.

Mysterious, but true. Remember what Dan Gottlieb says. Metaphor speaks—not always clearly, not always directly, but always powerfully.

Let's try a poem of six lines, with a simile in it, by the Japanese poet Ono no Komachi.

Doesn't he realize
that I am not
like the swaying kelp
in the surf,
where the seaweed gatherer
can come as often as he wants.

**Sounds as though that was written by a woman. She doesn't like the way "he" has has been treating her. He comes whenever he wants, like the seaweed gatherer.**

Sounds good to me, DR. You're getting the hang of this. Ready for a metaphor? Here is a poem by Imogene Bolls.

**DO IT**

### Coyote Wind

Scratching at the window
with claws of pine,
the wind wants in.

For days it has been
calling itself across
the white land, howling
on the hills, prowling
on the porch, crouching
hungry behind the barn.

When I turn on the light
it yelps, streaks off
across the yard, snow
covering its tracks,

It will be back.
It smells warm flesh
behind this frosted glass.

Just now it whimpers
in a corner of the porch
nursing a sore paw.

It knows all the tricks.

I won't open the door.

**I.Q.** **I know something's happening—but what is it? I mean, the wind doesn't really do things like that, so I know there's a metaphor.**

That's a good way to start. When a poem starts talking funny—acting as though things happen that don't—look for a metaphor. (As if the fog really *did* come in on little cat's feet.)

 **But what's the metaphor? Is it comparing the wind and a coyote? Something weird is going on. The wind will be back. It knows all the tricks. It yelps at the light. The speaker won't open the door. There's a lot of fear in there. So am I right if I say the poem is about fear?**

Say that the poem is *exploring* fear. I hate to think poems are only *about* things.

 **Okay. Is the poem *exploring* fear?**

Sounds good to me. Fear is in there. Read the poem over from that viewpoint. We'll wait.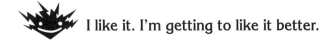

**I like it. I'm getting to like it better.**

Then I'd say your idea about the metaphor is starting to work. Keep reading and thinking about it. You'll see how good, how true, that poem is.

By the way, it's a poem with wonderful, gentle line breaks. Read the following aloud, pausing gently (with that little expectant rise in your voice), just as we learned last chapter.

For days it has been
calling itself across
the white land, howling
on the hills, prowling
on the porch, crouching
hungry behind the barn.

Now here it is in prose:

**For days it has been calling itself across the white land, howling on the hills, prowling on the porch, crouching hungry behind the barn.**

 Something is different with the prose version. It's pretty, all right, but you lose something.

Right. If you don't pause after "across"—

 The land doesn't seem as huge somehow. I don't know why, but it doesn't.

Maybe because we're waiting to hear across *what*?

 Maybe. "The white land" is sort of the payoff after the break.

Good, DR, very good. But what is the difference between "howling on the hills, prowling on the porch" and

>               howling
> on the hills, prowling
> on the porch?

 The first one makes me think of *where* it's all happening—the hills and the porch—but the line breaks in the poetry rearrange the rhythm and redirect my attention. That makes me think of the coyote (or wind) howling and prowling. The rhyme (nice one) helps you see it too. Hey—the line breaks and the rhymes are working together. How does she *do* that?

And feel how those lines build up tension? You have *howling*, then *prowling*, then *crouching*.

 First it makes a noise, then it starts to move, and now it's about to *do something*.

You can't rest, not until the last line. "Hungry behind the barn" lets us finally relax after that long (six whole lines!) build-up. Maybe that was what made you feel the fear, DR. I'd be afraid of anything crouching hungry behind the barn.

 **Wow. So the meaning of the words works with the pauses and the rhymes and the line breaks. This is turning out to be a really good poem.**

You're helping me prove two things: (**a**) that we should pay attention to pauses and line breaks, and (**b**) that poetry gets its effects both from words and from a whole host of elements beyond the words. The more attention you can pay, the better your experience will be.

Two more poems, and our workout will be over for today. Time for The Long Jump—from four lines to nine. I like to read Theodore Roethke aloud for his music. His poem "Root Cellar" describes a basement in which someone has left boxes full of bulbs and roots. The whole place is overgrown. When you read aloud, let your mouth get into the oral acrobatics. It's fun, and it *takes* you there.

Nothing would sleep in that cellar, dank as a ditch,
Bulbs broke out of boxes hunting for chinks in the dark,
Shoots dangled and drooped,
Lolling obscenely from mildewed crates,
Hung down long yellow evil necks, like tropical snakes.
And what a congress of stinks!—
Roots ripe as old bait,
Pulpy stems, rank, silo-rich,
Leaf-mold, manure, lime, piled against slippery planks.
Nothing would give up life:
Even the dirt kept breathing a small breath.

This poem is a symphony of vowels. Emphasize them as you read. For the line "Lolling obscenely from mildewed crates," get your nose and tongue into those *o*s, *i*s, and *a*s. Work your jaw John Wayne-style while drawling "Roots ripe as old bait." There's humor in the "congress of stinks," which you might find in Washington as well as in a cellar, and the last two lines are startling. Pleasure above all, but pleasure leads us to truth.

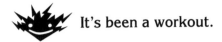 **It's been a workout.**

If you're worn out, save this last one for tomorrow. But if you're ambitious, try a sonnet by Robert Frost. The same rules of reading apply. "The Silken Tent" compares a woman to a tent of silk on a summer day.

She is as in a field a silken tent
At midday when a sunny summer breeze
Has dried the dew and all its ropes relent,
So that in guys it gently sways at ease,
And its supporting central cedar pole,
That is its pinnacle to heavenward
And signifies the sureness of the soul,
Seems to owe naught to any single cord,
But strictly held by none, is loosely bound
By countless silken ties of love and thought
To everything on earth the compass round,
And only by one's going slightly taut
In the capriciousness of summer air
Is of the slightest bondage made aware.

It's all one sentence, DR, so those pauses are important. The whole thing is one long, detailed comparison—the pleasure lies in working that comparison out.

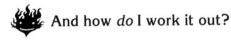 **And how *do* I work it out?**

Speculate, my dear DR. How might a woman resemble a tent like this? How might she be "loosely bound / By countless silken ties of love and thought"? Do you know any women like this? Are you one? Would you like to be?

# Day Two: The Ten-Mile Sprint

Welcome to Day Two. Let's warm up.

*One Line:*

I am what was, what is, what will be; no mortal has lifted my veil.

An ancient Greek inscription, spoken by Nature. Read it aloud. Get into it. Pretend you are Nature.

If that line doesn't give you a shiver, I'm sorry for you.

*Two Lines:*

Son, why are you weeping? Where does it hurt?
Tell me, and we'll know it together.

A mother to her weeping son, from Homer.

 **We'll *know* it together. I love that.**

Once more, with feeling.  We'll wait.

*Three Lines:*

Thus I
Pass by,
And die.

That's from "Upon My Departure" by Robert Herrick. Make sure you get those pauses in, because the poem doesn't last too long.

Hup-la! Six lines, then, from Alfred, Lord Tennyson:

### The Eagle: A Fragment

He clasps the crag with crooked hands;
Close to the sun in lonely lands,
Ringed with the azure world, he stands.

The wrinkled sea beneath him crawls;
He watches from his mountain walls,
And like a thunderbolt he falls.

Remember how we said poetry is a way to pay attention? No? Okay. Poetry is a way to pay attention.

See that word *clasps*? As part of our workout today, I want you to say every sound in it, please. Not the North American way—*he clastha cragwth crookid hanz.* Pay attention to what the words actually are, and actually say their actual sounds. After *clasps*, you will have to reset your mouth for the *th* in *the*. So try just those two words:

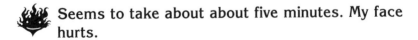

clasps the

Say them five times in a row, slowly.

Just to test your dedication—say them again five times, slowly, gently. We'll wait.

**Seems to take about about five minutes. My face hurts.**

Now, with the same gentle attention, read the whole line. Don't exaggerate. Just let every word have its own momentary space:

He clasps the crag with crooked hands

Now read all six lines in the same way. If you do, you'll see how good those lines are.

Now—not to flog this little poem to utter death—notice that the last three lines build up tension. You have that wrinkled sea crawling—and by the end, that thunderbolt. Voop! A release, if ever there was one. Try to read so that the tension builds just before the eagle strikes.

A fine sweat is now covering your healthy body. Let's vault to a poem of twenty-four whole lines, by Deborah Pope.

### Getting Through

Like a car stuck in gear,
a chicken too stupid to tell
its head is gone,
or sound ratcheting on
long after the film
has jumped the reel,
or a phone
ringing and ringing
in the house they have all
moved away from,
through rooms where dust
is a deepening skin,
and the locks unneeded,
so I go on loving you,
my heart blundering on,
a muscle spilling out
what is no longer wanted,
and my words hurtling past,
like a train off its track,
toward a boarded-up station,
closed for years,
like some last speaker
of a beautiful language
no one else can hear.

How many similes can you count in that poem?

About six. A couple of metaphors in there, too. Question: Who is the "they" in that bit about the house? It sounds like we're supposed to know them.

Well, you do. List all the things you know about them.

Okay . . . They're not at home . . . haven't been for a while, because the house is dusty. No one would want to break in, I guess, because it says that "locks" are "unneeded" . . .

Good attention-paying!

 . . . and the phone's ringing. There is nobody to pick it up. It's mysterious. And sad. And sort of hopeless.

Like?

 Like her love for this guy.

There's your metaphor. It pays to work metaphors out. The speaker says her words are "hurtling past, / like a train off its track, / toward a boarded-up station, / closed for years." So what does the boarded-up station stand for?

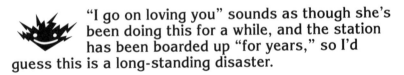 I knew you were going to ask me that.

Be patient. No Need to Rush. My words are like a train, and that train is going somewhere. Where do words usually go?

To somebody else. Oh, all right, so the boarded-up station is somebody else—okay, okay—it's the person she's in love with! That person doesn't love her and can't hear her.

Is this a recent development or a long-standing one?

"I go on loving you" sounds as though she's been doing this for a while, and the station has been boarded up "for years," so I'd guess this is a long-standing disaster.

 Good work, DR. It pays to pay attention.

BINGO!

# Day Three: Situation, Speaker, and Setting

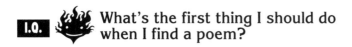

**I.Q.** What's the first thing I should do when I find a poem?

Read it. That will be twenty dollars, please. Seriously, read it through. You won't get all of it—ever. (Poems can't be exhausted. Otherwise we would never reread them.) Last chapter we mentioned that all poems have a **speaker**—the person "speaking" the words of the poem. With that in mind, ask three questions at the outset:

☞ Who is doing the speaking here?

☞ What is the *situation?*

☞ What are the speaker's feelings about that situation?

You should figure out those three things even before you look for a subject or a theme. Sometimes the speaker is involved personally, sometimes not. Here's an example of an involved speaker, in an epigram by John Gay.

**My Own Epitaph**

Life is a jest; and all things show it.
I thought so once; but now I know it.

What's the situation here?

In the ground, that's the situation. The title gives the game away. The speaker is dead. Not dead serious, though, not totally.

Here's another one, by William Carlos Williams.

**This Is Just to Say**

I have eaten
the plums
that were in
the icebox

43

and which
you were probably
saving
for breakfast

Forgive me
they were delicious
so sweet
and so cold

**I.Q.** *That's* **a poem?**

Many people think so. Read it through again and try to figure out the situation. We'll wait.

 **Sounds like a note you'd leave on the fridge.**

Evidently that's just what it was. Pay attention to what you know and piece it all together.

 **You got it.**
  • **The "you" was saving those plums for break-fast, probably.**
  • **The "I" (the speaker) ate them. The pig.**
  • **Maybe he came home late and was hungry. Maybe she was asleep, and he wrote the note for her to find when she woke up. So when he writes it, maybe he's smiling, thinking about her being asleep while he smoggled up all the plums, and about her face when she finds the note.**

So that's your situation. How does the speaker feel about this situation?

 **He's sorry—but not that sorry.**

What do you mean? He was considerate enough to write "you" a note about the entire affair.

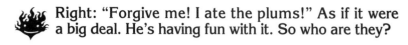

**Right:** "Forgive me! I ate the plums!" As if it were a big deal. He's having fun with it. So who are they?

The speaker is playful. And loving. We can tell there is intimacy between the speaker and the "you."

 **I say it's a man and his wife.**

**Bull's-eye!** Story goes that this poem was indeed a note left on the kitchen table or icebox for Williams's wife to find. He ate the plums, penned the poem, and, I guess, went to bed. Instant fame.

Speaker, situation, and setting are three big keys to any poem. In T. S. Eliot's "The Love Song of J. Alfred Prufrock," a disappointed man speaks about his disappointment. He seems to be at a party or social get-together of some kind: "In the room the women come and go / Talking of Michelangelo." That speaker, his situation, and the time and place he's in, are important in Eliot, and in "Hitting Golfballs off the Bluff" (page 54)—or "Getting Through" (page 41). Situation, speaker, and setting, baby.

Sometimes poems are so simple that you really have to *stay alert* to piece things together. I think you are ready for twelve lines, not too long, by Robert Creeley.

**I Know a Man**

As I sd to my
friend, because I am
always talking,—John, I

sd, which was not his
name, the darkness sur-
rounds us, what

can we do against
it, or else, shall we &
why not, buy a goddamn big car,

drive, he sd, for
christ's sake, look
out where yr going.

**Please tell me I can stop now. What is going on in this poem?**

It's in pretty simple English, DR. As far as I know, *sd* is *said,* & is *and*, and *yr* is *your.*

 **Well . . . okay . . . I knew that.**

Creeley, sly fellow, has mixed up the punctuation and line breaks just enough so that you *have to slow down* and consider what is going on. Let's look at it in prose:

> **As I said to my friend (because I am always talking)—"John," I said (which was not his name), "the darkness surrounds us. What can we do against it? Or else, shall we—and why not!—buy a god-damn big car—"**
>
> **"Drive," he said. "For Christ's sake, look out where you're going."**

Now. Who is the speaker?

 **This person talking to a man who is not named John. That's weird, by the way. He (he sounds like a man to me) is driving a car and talking to his friend, not-John.**

How is he driving?

 **Not too well, because not-John tells him to look out where he's going. Not-John seems not too happy with him.**

True. Why is the speaker driving badly?

**I guess because he's talking so much. He says he's "always talking."**

What is he talking about?

**46**

About how "the darkness surrounds us."

Correction: how
     the darkness sur-
     rounds us.

 Right. That line break stretches out "sur-
rounds," so you get more of a surrounding
feeling.

So what does not-John think about this philosophical discussion?

 Not much, I guess, because if the
speaker/driver doesn't watch the road, they
could get killed.

So the moral of our story?

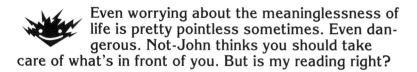 Even worrying about the meaninglessness of
life is pretty pointless sometimes. Even dan-
gerous. Not-John thinks you should take
care of what's in front of you. But is my reading right?

Sounds good to me. There might be more, but it's a pretty good
point.
    And now . . . time to take revenge.

## Revenge of the Audience

    Don't look now, but school's out. Is Mr. Pronk or Mrs. Van
Blort around to whack your earlobes if you miss the zeugma or
the asyndeton in Marvell's "To His Coy Mistress"? No? Then pay
'em back, that's what I say. Get out there, get yourself a poem, and

*. . . enjoy it.* Read it aloud and think anything you want about it. You may be right, you may be wrong, but you won't be graded. Here. Have a poem, Robert Frost's "Dust of Snow."

The way a crow
Shook down on me
The dust of snow
From a hemlock tree

Has given my heart
A change of mood
And saved some part
Of a day I had rued.

Man, do you need the heavy intellectual guns for that one or what? The speaker was feeling blue, some crow shook snow on him, and for some nice reason, yours to discover, it cheered him up. Class dismissed.

Your homework: One night, instead of going to your usual vampire/buddy cops/car-crash/writhing bodies flick, take in a poetry reading. Go in, take a seat, and, with mind and heart engaged, listen to a few poets. There are wide variations in quality—and be prepared not to like some of what you hear. On the whole, however, poets are usually pretty good at reading. Some of them even get paid to do it.

If you absolutely can't stand it, catch the late movie. But like it or not, try it more than once. Bring friends. Talk about what you liked and what you didn't.

Have friends read poems aloud to you. And listen, DR. Organize reading circles. Sometimes look at the poem while your friends are reading; other times close your eyes and listen; other times open your eyes and listen.

Now here's the big one. Bring some poetry home with you. Maybe not on the first date, but once you get to like each other. It is possible to buy four or five poetry books for less than $30. You can buy volumes (even new) by Wendell Berry, Pablo Neruda,

Adrienne Rich, and William Shakespeare for less than $25. And they're free at the library.

Position your new books at strategic places around the house—not where you won't read (coffee table, bookshelf) but where you might (on the kitchen table; next to the phone; on the TV tray, between the nachos and the beer; on the nightstand; on the bathroom sink, he wrote euphemistically).

Put a book next to your microwave. While you're standing there waiting for the baby's bottle or your tea, instead of muttering "60 . . . 59 . . . 58" with the display, read aloud. I've seen people tape poems to the refrigerator.

And I must say I have high hopes for the bathroom.

People are desperate; they'll read *anything* in there.

Instead of the article in *People* that you have begun thirty-eight times, try a book of poems that, if you're lucky, might fall open almost anywhere.

If friends come over and say, "Why are you reading this stuff?," make fun of them for not getting with the latest national culture movement. Maybe you'll start a chain reaction.

From time to time, pick up a book and read a few lines. Look for short poems and read them aloud. Not at 2:00 a.m. when your bedmate is snoring, but whenever possible.

Many poems that look ghostly on the page take on flesh and blood when you give them voice. Give them voice.

If thy book afflict thee, close it and select another. Add and subtract titles. As you go along, you'll be building your personal tastes and standards.

The idea is to adopt poetry as a live alternative for your entertainment moment. No one expects you to give up TV. But when your TV fails you, think of poetry. When the video store shelves are bare, when you've surfed through all 550 channels and found nothing on (not unusual), when you've channel-surfed some more (I know you), hit Mute or Off, pick up a book of poems, and read a few lines aloud. If you like those, read a few more aloud.

Take revenge on a lifetime of prejudice and bad advice. Try it. You'll like it.

You've got your poetry legs. Now you are a whippet-quick, wide-eyed reader, ready for anything.

**Chapter Three:**

# getting the good stuff, or what you can learn from poems

**Y**ou actually can learn a great deal from poetry.

**I.Q.** What? Come on. Poetry has no practical value, no place in the real world of technology, multinational realignment, the Human Genome Project, and sneakers with taillights!

*Au contraire, Cher Lecteur.* My point is not that *POETRY HAS FAX U CAN USE!* True, many poems can give you information and skills you previously lacked, if that is what you want. Here is a poem by Ted Kooser, one that taught me something.

### How to Make Rhubarb Wine

Go to the patch some afternoon
in early summer, fuzzy with beer
and sunlight, and pick a sack
of rhubarb (red or green will do)
and God knows watch for rattlesnakes
or better, listen; they make a sound
like an old lawnmower rolled downhill.
Wear a hat. A straw hat's best
for the heat but lets the gnats in.
Bunch up the stalks and chop the leaves off
with a buck-knife and be careful.
You need ten pounds; a grocery bag
packed full will do it. Then go home
and sit barefooted in the shade
behind the house with a can of beer.
Spread out the rhubarb in the grass
and wash it with cold water
from the garden hose, washing

your feet as well. Then take a nap.
That evening, dice the rhubarb up
and put it in a crock. Then pour
eight quarts of boiling water in,
cover it up with a checkered cloth
to keep the fruit flies out of it,
and let it stand five days or so.
Take time each day to think of it.

When the time is up, dip out the pulp
with your hands for strainers; leave the juice.
Stir in five pounds of sugar
and an envelope of Red Star yeast.

Ferment ten days, under the cloth,
sniffing of it from time to time,
then siphon it off, swallowing some,
and bottle it. Sit back and watch
the liquid clear to honey-yellow,
bottled and ready for the years,
and smile. You've done it awfully well.

**BINGO!** You bet! I went off and did just as he said, and it works. The nap is the important thing.

(Isn't that just a delightful poem?)

So yes, you can find poems with factual information. Now you know how to make rhubarb wine. When I say, "You can learn from poems," however, I mean something slightly different. Not the way you learn from textbooks—rather, the way you learn from hearing people talk about their lives. And from living your own life.

That means **poetry is a repository of experience and wisdom**.

**BINGO!** You bet. We think of science and religion and ethics and your-pick-here as addressing the facts of life. And they do! But make room for poetry, which has always been there—since the beginning of writing and probably before, through song and stories.

Suppose you want to know what it's like for a woman to love her husband. Perhaps you love yours. Perhaps you don't, or wish you did. Maybe you are or wish to be a husband, and wonder what the other side is thinking and feeling. There is always "How do I love thee? Let me count the ways," which Elizabeth Barrett Browning wrote around the time she eloped with Robert Browning.

But you know that one, so how about this, by Mistress Anne Bradstreet (1612–1672), one of America's very first poets?

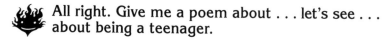

### To My Dear and Loving Husband

If ever two were one, then surely we.
If ever man were lov'd by wife, then thee.
If ever wife was happy in a man,
Compare with me, ye women, if you can.
I prize thy love more than whole Mines of gold,
Or all the riches that the East doth hold.
My love is such that Rivers cannot quench,
Nor ought but love from thee give recompense.
Thy love is such I can no way repay;
The heavens reward thee manifold I pray.
Then while we live, in love let's so persever,
That when we live no more, we may live ever.

She is not the most sophisticated poet in the world—rhyming *quench* and *recompense* is a stretch. But how charming this little poem is, how open and hopeful.

Throughout history—but especially in the past century—people have been writing about their lives, the facts of their lives, and how their lives felt to them. Call it the **Subjective Truth**—an important kind. We see the world through the camera of someone else's eyes.

**All right. Give me a poem about . . . let's see . . . about being a teenager.**

You're on. A good subject, tough to write about. Jeffrey Harrison is here to help us.

## Hitting Golfballs off the Bluff

They come back now, those nights my friend and I
hit golfballs off the bluff behind his house.
We were sixteen and had our learner's permits
but no girlfriends, unlike the football jocks
we couldn't stand but secretly envied.
Neither of us actually played golf,
but late one night we took his father's clubs
and started what became a ritual.
A Freudian would have a field day with it:
the clubs, the balls, the deep ravine below
with train tracks and a river running through it.
But for us it was pure exhilaration:
the sure feel of a good connection, zing
of the white ball disappearing into blackness,
then silence as we waited for the thud
against the ground below, splash in the river,
or bang against the roof of a freight car.
That drawn-out moment when we only listened,
holding our laughter back, seemed never-ending
and one time was: no sound came back at all,
as if we'd sent the golfball into orbit
like a new planet—one we might still see
moving across the sky on any night,
pocked like the moon, but smaller, shining green
with envy now, now deep red with desire.

**BINGO!** Uh huh! You bet!

# The Work Life

   People write about their work lives all the time—insurance
executives, bankers, doctors, truck drivers, ranchers, conve-
nience-store clerks, janitors, SCUBA divers, circus clowns,
nurses, and accountants. This poetry of work is one of the great
treasures we have. One example is "What Work Is," by the Detroit-

born poet Philip Levine. It takes in work, all right, also brothers and their love. As soon as it was printed, it became permanent.

We stand in the rain a long line
waiting at Ford Highland Park. For work.
You know what work is—if you're
old enough to read this you know what
work is, although you may not do it.
Forget you. This is about waiting,
shifting from one foot to another.
Feeling the light rain falling like mist
into your hair, blurring your vision
until you think you see your own brother
ahead of you, maybe ten places.
You rub your glasses with your fingers,
and of course it's someone else's brother,
narrower across the shoulders than
yours but with the same sad slouch, the grin
that does not hide the stubbornness,
the sad refusal to give in to
rain, to the hours wasted waiting,
to the knowledge that somewhere ahead
a man is waiting who will say, "No,
we're not hiring today," for any
reason he wants. You love your brother,
now suddenly you can hardly stand
the love flooding you for your brother,
who's not beside you or behind or
ahead because he's home trying to
sleep off a miserable night shift
at Cadillac so he can get up
before noon to study his German.
Works eight hours a night so he can sing
Wagner, the opera you hate most,
the worst music ever invented.
How long has it been since you told him
you loved him, held his wide shoulders,
opened your eyes wide and said those words,

and maybe kissed his cheek? You've never
done something so simple, so obvious,
not because you're too young or too dumb,
not because you're jealous or even mean
or incapable of crying in
the presence of another man, no,
just because you don't know what work is.

There is wisdom and pure, hard experience packed in a small space. I learn and learn from reading this poem aloud. If you want to learn about other people's lives, you know where to go.

 **Got it. But is that really poetry? I mean, it's almost like someone just talking to you. It's so much like ordinary talk.**

So? Ordinary talk has poetry in it. There's a famous poem by Michael Drayton, a contemporary of Shakespeare, that sounds like a lover talking to his/her soon-to-be ex, in that formal, angry way breakers-up break up.

Since there's no help, come let us kiss and part;
Nay, I have done, you get no more of me
(Sonnet 61)

You get no more of me, baby. You better remember this good stuff cuz there ain't no more after this. Gimme a kiss and ramble. Straight talk can make poetry. Why not? Here, have some more straight talk, from Joe Heithaus.

### Butcher's Son

Nothing to do with blood. Nineteen,
I cut off my left pinky and he laughed, held
my bleeding hand over the chopping block
beside four sides of beef on hooks.
*He's a butcher today* he must have thought, his own
missing pointer scratching his head. He smiled,
walked me to the sink, the light at the door
was gray, the cat pawed a kidney behind the screen.

I thought of all this at my wedding when he held
up my hand after the mass—four fingers
and stump, the gold ring, Amy staring down
at her dress. It was '69, Vietnam, Nixon
president, we drove away in a big black Electra
and talked about my buddies overseas who
couldn't be there, his insistence we bring
a cooler of steaks on the honeymoon.

When I remember those days, I hate him.
That fucking back room, the sawdust
I've swept every day since I turned sixteen.
*Joey, help Mrs. Benson, sharpen this knife,*
and she'd whisper, *What a sweet man
your father is.* I'd fake a smile, look
out the window at the theatre across the street.

We're closed today, I'm putting my black suit
back on, scrubbing the stains from my hands.

Looking into other people's lives this intimately can be very
hard. This bears the stamp of experience. The best poetry doesn't
turn away from life but looks it straight in the snoot. In "Butcher's
Son," I like how the little details carry a great deal of weight. Amy
stares down at her dress.

 **So you know that she and the father don't get
along so well.**

The speaker stares at the "theatre across the street"—perhaps he
is dreaming of something better, a way out of the dead-end life his
father has arranged for him. Details hurt—the cat pawing the kid-
ney, the cooler of steaks—

Yeah—his dad horning in, even on their honey-moon.

And of course, the pinky.

## Solace

Over the millennia, people have used poetry for solace. Comfort. Poets write about the great moments in life—and many of those are filled with doubt, pain, and suffering.

A few poems give solace by suggesting solutions to problems. Others comfort us by presenting a healing point of view, or by setting our suffering in context. It's a comfort to hear someone else speak of a situation similar to ours.

But, as a friend of mine puts it, poems comfort us most often "by just saying it." Poets are good at setting down a crystal-clear, emotionally affecting picture of what it is like to suffer pain, lose a loved one, face death, loneliness, or fear.

Poems, DR, are full of wisdom—knowledge of life gained through experience. Wisdom is well known for giving comfort. It makes things clear, reminds us of things we've forgotten, gives us a bigger perspective.

 **That reminds me of something I wanted to bring up. Notice how many of these poems actually are bigger than the things they're talking about?**

You mean they transcend their subject matter.

 **Now I know why you wrote this book. But that poem "What Work Is," that's also speaking about love and sympathy.**

Life is hard, but people really do love each other.

 **Exactly. That "Butcher's Son" poem has a lot to say about hope and despair. And the golfballs poem is suggesting how life sometimes is crazier and more mysterious than you could invent.**

Very good point, DR. What you say is true about paintings, sculpture, and music, too. Art comforts us with its power to suggest much larger meanings; it has a way of getting us to take a—what's a good word?—

 **Transcendent.**

—transcendent point of view. Transcendence is comforting. It takes you out of your own boundaries, your own experience. It opens you up. People need that. The comfort of transcendence happens in even the humblest of poems.

## Loneliness

Loneliness is a gnawing kind of pain very close to grief. There are many poems on loneliness, one of the best being this one by Vikram Seth.

### All You Who Sleep Tonight

All you who sleep tonight
Far from the ones you love,
No hand to left or right,
And emptiness above—

Know that you aren't alone.
The whole world shares your tears,
Some for two nights or one,
And some for all their years.

What is comforting—besides knowing that others share your situation—is the poem's simplicity, the power of just saying it.

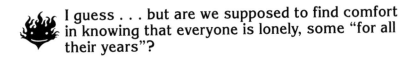 I guess . . . but are we supposed to find comfort in knowing that everyone is lonely, some "for all their years"?

Sometimes that's the best you can get. But if you want another view of loneliness, here is Adrienne Rich.

## Song

You're wondering if I'm lonely:
OK then, yes, I'm lonely
as a plane rides lonely and level
on its radio beam, aiming
across the Rockies
for the blue-strung aisles
of an airfield on the ocean

You want to ask, am I lonely?
Well, of course, lonely
as a woman driving across country
day after day, leaving behind
mile after mile
little towns she might have stopped
and lived and died in, lonely

If I'm lonely
it must be the loneliness
of waking first, of breathing
dawn's first cold breath on the city
of being the one awake
in a house wrapped in sleep

If I'm lonely
it's with the rowboat ice-fast on the shore
in the last red light of the year
that knows what it is, that knows it's neither
ice nor mud nor winter light
but wood, with a gift for burning

## BINGO!

 A calm, quiet poem. Sure, the four similes—with the plane, the woman, the person waking first, the rowboat—are beautiful in odd, unexpected ways. But what I like is how *positive* a poem this is. That plane has somewhere to get to, in the vast Western sky.

## So does the woman driving the car.

**You bet.** The third stanza is simply magical. And that 4:30 p.m. December 31st rowboat, with its "gift for burning"! Maybe there is a strength in loneliness, an integrity. I admire the speaker, who is lonely, but in good, strong ways.

# Parting

To part with a beloved friend, lover, place, thing—what could be more spiritually rending? Thousands of years before "Parting is such sweet sorrow," poets were writing about it. Let's say you are a father seeing his daughter off at the airport, as Yvor Winters once was.

### At the San Francisco Airport
*To my daughter, 1954*

This is the terminal: the light
Gives perfect vision, false and hard;
The metal glitters, deep and bright.
Great planes are waiting in the yard—
They are already in the night.

And you are here beside me, small,
Contained and fragile, and intent
On things that I but half recall—
Yet going whither you are bent.
I am the past, and that is all.

But you and I in part are one:
The frightened brain, the nervous will,
The knowledge of what must be done,
The passion to acquire the skill
To face that which you dare not shun.

The rain of matter upon sense
Destroys me momently. The score:
There comes what will come. The expense
Is what one thought, and something more—
One's being and intelligence.

This is the terminal, the break.
Beyond this point, on lines of air,
You take the way that you must take;
And I remain in light and stare—
In light, and nothing else, awake.

**BINGO!** Winters's poem doesn't turn away from the pain (he even lets it destroy him for a moment); rather, it depicts the courage and strength to continue with life even though a part of it is gone forever. He and his daughter are one in many ways—including the knowledge that they must part, take different directions, take the ways they must take.

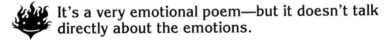 It's a very emotional poem—but it doesn't talk directly about the emotions.

**Yes**—as with most good poems, Winters has set up the situation so well that he doesn't *have* to tell you what he's feeling; you'll do the feeling by yourself.

There's another poem that transcends its boundaries. The word *terminal* means the airport terminal, but also it means an ending. It makes you think of other endings in life.

You can feel the pain of parting, and the courage of the speaker, so "awake" in the light of the last lines. Both he and his daughter will bear up and bear on. If you experience this poem fully, you'll bring it—and its lessons, and their comfort—along with you for years.

# Aging

The past century has seen many fine poems about aging: what's bad, what's good, what's next. W. B. Yeats has a few of the best lines ever written about old men.

> An aged man is but a paltry thing,
> A tattered coat upon a stick, unless
> Soul clap its hands and sing, and louder sing
> For every tatter in its mortal dress
>> ("Sailing to Byzantium")

Read those lines aloud, DR. Like all of Yeats, they resound with music. Also, it's a good point—if you are going to be old, might as well clap your hands and sing, all the louder because you are a little tattered.

Today's poets write many poems about themselves aging—and about seeing others age. I like the poems that, hopeful or hopeless, end somehow with a sense of dignity and worth. One of these is by John Updike.

### Elderly Sex

> Life's buried treasure's buried deeper still:
> a cough, a draft, a wrinkle in the bed
> distract the search, as precarious as
> a safecracker's trembling touch on the dial.
> We are walking a slack tight wire, we
> are engaged in unlikely acrobatics,
> we are less frightened of the tiger than
> of the possibility the cage is empty.
>
> Nature used to do more—paroxysms
> of blood and muscle, the momentous machine
> set instantly in place, the dark a-swim,
> and lubrication's thousand jewels poured forth
> by lapfuls where, with dry precision, now
> attentive irritation yields one pearl.

I think the poem is relentless, heartbreaking, and affirmative.

 **How are we supposed to get comfort from that?**

Let's talk. Remember "Song" by Adrienne Rich? Comfort came from her sense that we can remain strong, with a "gift for burning" we keep even when we feel lonely. Something similar was true with "At the San Francisco Airport" by Yvor Winters and with "All You Who Sleep Tonight" by Vikram Seth. In Updike's poem, two old people make love, and it isn't what it used to be. It isn't as good, as powerful, as sex was when they were younger.

That's sad, no doubt about it. But, DR, there *is* a treasure at the end, to be gained by "attentive" work. Despite the losses of time, people are trying to be good to (and for) each other. Updike doesn't smooth over the awkwardness of it all (that "wrinkle in the bed"); instead, he reminds us that people need intimacy and can help each other. We come away feeling sad and hopeful at the same time—very sad, maybe, but still hopeful.

 **So hope is more powerful when you're not fooling yourself? When you see the facts, feel the pain, and still find the good stuff?**

Could be! Poems can point out the possibilities for hope. But we have to be ready to feel different combinations of emotions—sadness *and* comfort, hope *and* hopelessness, joy *and* irony. Just as you do in real life. Reality is full of **ambiguity**, DR, and it makes you feel **ambivalence**, which can be a very productive state of mind.

Here's another poem on aging, by Shakespeare. To me, this is one of the most comforting poems ever written. Please, please, please read this one aloud, with tender attention.

DO **IT**

### Sonnet 73

That time of year thou mayst in me behold
When yellow leaves, or none, or few, do hang
Upon those boughs which shake against the cold,
Bare ruined choirs, where late the sweet birds sang.
In me thou see'st the twilight of such day
As after sunset fadeth in the west;

Which by and by black night doth take away,
Death's second self, that seals up all in rest.
In me thou see'st the glowing of such fire,
That on the ashes of his youth doth lie,
As the deathbed whereon it must expire,
Consumed with that which it was nourished by.
This thou perceiv'st, which makes thy love more strong,
To love that well which thou must leave ere long.

My friend sees me aging, and loves me more—knowing I'll soon be gone. This poem builds up by focusing down—from a season to an evening to a fire. By the way, remember we were speaking about meter *versus* rhythm? This sonnet is in good old iambic pentameter. Try reading the following line aloud as a regular duh DAH duh DAH duh DAH duh DAH duh DAH:

as THE deathBED whereON it MUST exPIRE

What do you think?

 **It stinks.**

True. The line almost **demands** to be read

AS the DEATHBED whereon it MUST exPIRE

Here's one more poem about aging, by the marvelous American poet Lucille Clifton.

there is a girl inside.
she is randy as a wolf.
she will not walk away
and leave these bones
to an old woman.

she is a green tree
in a forest of kindling.
she is a green girl
in a used poet.

she has waited
patient as a nun
for the second coming,
when she can break through gray hairs
into blossom

and her lovers will harvest
honey and thyme
and the woods will be wild
with the damn wonder of it.

Clap your hands and sing. There is both sorrow and celebration.
Old? Yes, she's getting old. But the girl is alive inside.

## Fear Itself

As we've seen, poetry often faces our biggest fears with
courage. May Swenson writes about a fear we all have. Throughout
the whole poem, from beginning to end, her speaker is afraid. But
she's facing it, and she makes something out of her fear.

### Night Practice

I
will
remember
with my breath
to make a mountain,
with my sucked-in breath
a valley, with my pushed-out
breath a mountain. I will make
a valley wider than the whisper, I
will make a higher mountain than the cry;
will with my will breathe a mountain, I will
with my will breathe a valley. I will push out
a mountain, suck in a valley, deeper than the shout
YOU MUST DIE, harder, heavier, sharper, a mountain than
the truth YOU MUST DIE. I will remember, My breath will
make a mountain. My will will remember to will. I, suck-
ing, pushing, I will breathe a valley, I will breathe a mountain.

That's called **concrete poetry**—when a poem is shaped like the thing it's about. Can you see the comfort in this poem?

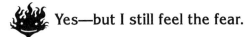 **Yes—but I still feel the fear.**

It can be a courageous thing simply to breathe.

## Belief, Unbelief, and Beyond

Religious belief is one of the most comforting things in the world—and one of the most painful. Unbelief is one of the worst sufferings people can have—and one of the strongest comforts. Poets have written millions of poems on belief and un-. Along with love, the God thing is probably the all-time Topic Number One.

Alfred, Lord Tennyson's poem *In Memoriam* wrestles with the angel of doubt for hundreds of stanzas. He comes up with belief earned through suffering.

**DO** **IT**

That which we dare invoke to bless;
  Our dearest faith; our ghastliest doubt;
  He, They, One, All; within, without;
The Power in darkness whom we guess;

I found Him not in world or sun,
  Or eagle's wing, or insect's eye;
  Nor through the questions men may try,
The petty cobwebs we have spun:

If e'er when faith had fallen asleep,
  I heard a voice, "believe no more"
  And heard an ever-breaking shore
That tumbled in the Godless deep;

A warmth within the breast would melt
  The freezing reason's colder part,
  And like a man in wrath the heart
Stood up and answered, "I have felt."

No, like a child in doubt and fear:
  But that blind clamor made me wise;
  Then was I as a child that cries,
But, crying, knows his father near;

And what I am beheld again
  What is, and no man understands;
  And out of darkness came the hands
That reach through nature, molding men.

"Don't care what reason says—I know what I feel." Not a bad rejoinder, for all its warts. Though belief often isn't easy, what belief finds in the world is powerful. T. S. Eliot gets positively elevated about it.

Quick now, here, now, always—
A condition of complete simplicity
(Costing not less than everything)
And all shall be well and
All manner of thing shall be well
                    ("Little Gidding")

As for atheism, it doesn't have to be wintry and horrible—it might be good enough just to be **here** and loving it. Wallace Stevens wrote what a friend of mine calls "The Atheist's National Anthem," a poem titled "Sunday Morning." Here, Stevens suggests a sort of replacement-religion in which we adopt something akin to the ancient practice of sun worship.

Supple and turbulent, a ring of men
Shall chant in orgy on a summer morn
Their boisterous devotion to the sun,
Not as a god, but as a god might be,
Naked among them, like a savage source.

We worship the sun "not as a god, but as a god might be." (The sun is about as brilliant and powerful and life-sustaining as you can get, so it really *is* as a god might be.) We're going to die and that's all, and life is vital and glorious. There's solace in that.

 **So there's no God in that poem?**

There is, but not in the sky. In the poem a woman realizes that

> Divinity must live within herself:
> Passions of rain, or moods in falling snow;
> Grievings in loneliness, or unsubdued
> Elations when the forest blooms; gusty
> Emotions on wet roads on autumn nights;
> All pleasures and all pains

Isn't that lovely?

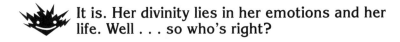 **It is. Her divinity lies in her emotions and her life. Well . . . so who's right?**

Wrong book. Our point is that poets take every imaginable stance on every imaginable issue, and they have drawn comfort both from there being a God in the universe and there being a divinity in themselves. Some, like Tennyson, vote for the afterlife. Some, like the woman in "Sunday Morning," vote for this life. Both offer comfort.

# Death

When we're at extremes, we go looking for poems. When we lose someone, we have several ways of seeking comfort. None of them works all the way, but all afford us a little help. One way is to see traces of our loved one in the world around us, as though he or she left these traces behind as a memento. Have some Robert Frost.

## Never Again Would Birds'
## Song Be the Same

He would declare and could himself believe
That the birds there in all the garden round
From having heard the daylong voice of Eve
Had added to their own an oversound,
Her tone of meaning but without the words.
Admittedly an eloquence so soft
Could only have had an influence on birds
When call or laughter carried it aloft.
Be that as may be, she was in their song.
Moreover her voice upon their voices crossed
Had now persisted in the woods so long
That probably it never would be lost.
Never again would birds' song be the same.
And to do that to birds was why she came.

You have "Eve," you have the "garden," and you have the unnamed "he," whom you could probably name. Eve is gone, but she made a difference.

# Advice

 **Do poems ever have actual advice in them? On how to live your life? How to make sense of it all?**

That's one of the oldest functions of poetry. And advice is certainly *implied* in many of the poems above. Poems are a kind of advice. Poets are people. People give other people advice. When advice comes in the form of poetry, it has staying power.

 **I mean the big kind of advice. How to see it all.**

It's one of the main things poems do. Here are two examples. The first is by Gary Snyder.

### For the Children

The rising hills, the slopes,
of statistics
lie before us.
the steep climb
of everything, going up,
up, as we all
go down.

In the next century
or the one beyond that,
they say,
are valleys, pastures,
we can meet there in peace
if we make it.

To climb these coming crests
one word to you, to
you and your children:

*stay together*
*learn the flowers*
*go light*

The wisdom of the ages in three lines. How are we going to "make it"? "Climb these coming crests"?

Each of his bits of advice means more than it says. To "*learn the flowers*" could mean to learn how the whole living world works. If we "*go light*," we won't weigh ourselves down—maybe with material things?

And "*stay together*" is—well, good advice.

One more poem, by the contemporary Greek poet C. P. Cavafy. This is one of my favorites. It is comforting and transcendent and full of advice. Ithaka was the home island of Odysseus in the *Odyssey*. It is the destination he's always trying to reach.

## Ithaka

Starting out on your journey to Ithaka,
Pray that your road is a long one,
Full of adventure, full of wisdom.
The Lestrygonians and Cyclops,
Furious Poseidon—don't fear them.
You won't meet anything like them on your way
so long as you keep your thoughts high
and an exquisite energy
kindles your soul and body.
Lestrygonians, Cyclops, savage Poseidon—
you'll never meet them unless
you carry them within,
unless your mind
holds them before you.

Pray that your road is a long one,
pray for many summer mornings
when, with such thankfulness! such joy!
you'll enter harbors you're
seeing for the first time ever.
May you stop at Phoenician trading posts
to purchase fine goods,
mother of pearl, coral, amber, ebony,
ravishing perfumes of every kind—
get as many ravishing perfumes as you can.
May you visit many Egyptian cities;
may you learn and learn from those who know.

Always keep your mind on Ithaka.
Getting there is your destiny—but
no need to rush. Better if getting there
lasts for many years, until, when you
drop anchor at the island,
you're old, rich
with all you've picked up along the way,
not expecting Ithaka to make you rich.

Ithaka has given you this wonderful journey.
Without her you wouldn't have started,
but she has nothing more to give.
And if you find her shabby, remember—
she won't have cheated you. By then,
with all the great wisdom, after all
the experience you've gained,
you will surely understand
what Ithaka means.

 **Now there's a metaphor.**

Sometimes paraphrase does injustice to a poem. You could say that the message here is "It's not the destination but the journey that's important," but the poem is more than that. It is full of enthusiasm for life and for plain old experience.

 **It's suggesting the best attitude to have for the journey. (Any journey, I guess, starting with the journey of life.) If you do it right, the ride is worth it.**

Keep your eyes on the goal, but get those ravishing perfumes.

**BINGO!**

# The Best Things Poetry Can Do For You

Here's the best you can hope for from poems.

Poetry can, through an act of the imagination, put you in someone else's shoes. And enjoying poetry is like anything else— the more you **DO** 🏃 **IT**, the better you get at it.

People used to say that poetry could make you a more moral person—sharpen your sense of other people's lives by presenting those lives in unforgettable truthfulness.

I think that's right. That's why I took it up. As you said, DR, poetry opens you up—to the world, to others, and (think of "Ithaka") to yourself. Transcendence, baby.

If poetry *is* a way of paying attention, then it could teach you how to pay attention to others. Could make you more aware. More understanding.

 Better.

BINGO!

Chapter Four:

# Old Stuff

We have a letter here from a future reader, and the letter goes something like this:

Dear John:

Shouldn't I be reading *old* stuff? *Really* old? You know—*thees* and *thous*? Shakespeare? And Milton? And—I guess this is my reason for writing—when I *do* read this really old stuff, aren't I just going to totally, totally ***hate*** it? Throw the book down, crash through the picture window, and go flying into the pool? Wonder (under water) why I am wasting my life? What this can possibly have to do with me? Why I bought your stupid book in the first place?

Please reply,
DR

First of all, picture windows cost a lot of money. Use a door. Secondly, our first point is that

☞ **You don't *have* to read anything. Read what you like to read.**

This feeling that you *have* to read Shakespeare is odd. Really. It has ruined thousands of lives. Even worse, it has probably ruined poetry for many, many people. I'd rather that you dabbled, hunted around, read many different kinds of poetry. See what's out there. Buy those ravishing perfumes.

I.Q.  But you don't really believe that, do you? You don't really think we shouldn't read Shakespeare. You're just trying to be a nice guy, right?

All right. I admit it. I am sitting here, drumming on my keyboard, experiencing distinct inner turmoil.

But DR, in a way, I do mean it.

You don't *have* to read anything. Reading something with galactically incredible advance notices—Shakespeare—is a tough assignment. He is so universally praised that it is hard to approach him with a clear mind and heart. You are already twice prejudiced—*against* Shakespeare for being so famous but not famous *to you*, and *against yourself*, for being stupid enough not to know or like him. Same for Milton, T. S. Eliot, Homer, the Psalms, Wordsworth.

 **Fine. We have a cultural complex. But what do you really think about this Shakespeare guy?**

I think that anyone who wants to read poetry *will* someday try Shakespeare.

 **Come on. Out with it.**

If you skip him, you're missing out, baby. What else do you want me to say?

I once had a teacher who talked about "The Shakespeare Machine." He explained it this way:

> **Ordinary Stuff Goes In and Comes Out Poetry.**

I believe in The Shakespeare Machine. The first Shakespeare I ever saw was a TV version of *Macbeth* starring Orson Welles. I was about nine. I stayed up with my dad. And you know what? I don't remember being especially mystified by the language. I understood what was going on, and I couldn't not watch. I also thought that the last part, where they brought in his head on a stick, was excellent.

Since then, I've felt at home with William S. He tells interesting stories. He can create hundreds of different characters—many of them entirely convincing. He's got range, too. He is one of the most profound of writers—and one of the funniest.

As a poet, well, even when he is not being very original, that old Shakespeare Machine grinds away. (How does he *do* that?) I figure he simply thought in metaphors, images, beautiful ways of saying things.

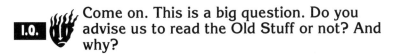 **You're depressing me. So we *do* have to read the Old Stuff?**

No! Thousands are leading innocent, happy lives without Shakespeare or any of the old poets.

**Come on. This is a big question. Do you advise us to read the Old Stuff or not? And why?**

Wait. I have to stop typing.

I'm back. I paced the house. Then I put on some clothes, showered, made breakfast, took out the trash. I pondered the question. Here is my answer:

**People have been writing poetry for at least five thousand years. The probability that you will like some of it is high.**

Think of all the good stuff out there. I know many people who, after putting up a fuss, let themselves get into a little bit of it—and they found out. Their lives are different, in a good way. Some are doctors and others are homemakers. A few are toxic waste site disposal engineers. But they have this extra dimension now. Yes— they are sitting down with their Homer or Vergil or Chaucer or Dante every once in a while. And after all these centuries, those cats are still meowing loud and clear. **We keep reading Old Stuff because it collects the best that has ever been said, thought, and felt about things we all say, think, and feel. And the treasure heap just keeps growing.**

 Advice?

Always. Read the rest of this chapter, and then peruse my *Appreciator's Guide* (page 85). Look up poets you've heard about, and see what I have to say. My main point with all these poets is this: *there are reasons people have loved them and love them still*. Getting at them can be work, but in many cases (Shakespeare and Dante are definitely two) it's more than worth it.

# Riding the Shakespeare Machine

Here's how I would approach Shakespeare.

☞ **Get over the language thing.** Yes, there will be *thee*s, *thou*s, and a few *wouldest*s. What can I say? When was the last time you read the headline *Thousands Murdered by Rampaging Thou*? They talked that way. Some still do. I myself was called "thou" when I lived in the north of England, as in "Where hast thou been, John?" by my boss. "Thou'rt fired" came later.

**Fact:** Shakespeare did not speak Old English.

He spoke Early Modern English—essentially the same language as ours, but with a different pronunciation, a somewhat different vocabulary, and a few grammatical holdovers from earlier versions of English.

But folks make too much of it. Yes, you can find passages such as

> Peace, I say! hear mine host of the Garter. Am I politic? Am I subtle? Am I a Machiavel? Shall I lose my doctor? No, he gives me the potions and the motions. Shall I lose my parson? My priest? My Sir Hugh? No, he gives me the proverbs and the no-verbs. Give me thy hand, terrestrial; so. Give me thy hand, celestial; so.

which appear to be in Urdo-Finnish. But this is *The Merry Wives of Windsor*, a play, and if you're watching the play (instead of merely reading it), you'll even understand most of the above.

You can also find passages like Petruchio's speech in *The Taming of the Shrew*:

> They shall go forward, Kate, at thy command.
> Obey the bride, you that attend on her.
> Go to the feast, revel and domineer,
> Carouse full measure to her maidenhead,
> Be mad and merry, or go hang yourselves;
> But for my bonny Kate, she must with me.
> Nay, look not big, nor stamp, nor stare, nor fret,
> I will be master of what is mine own.
> She is my goods, my chattels, she is my house,
> My household stuff, my field, my barn,
> My horse, my ox, my ass, my anything;
> And here she stands

So what's so hard here? Exactly once he says *mine* where we would say *my*—which Shakespeare sometimes did before words that start in vowels ("mine own"). Well, sue the guy. *She must with me* means *She must go with me*. (Sweat pops out on the brow!) And, oh God, stepping on cars, smashing elevated train lines, marauding and despoiling—a *thy!*

Most of Shakespeare is somewhere in between these two examples. The differences between him and us are small—mostly in vocabulary. Besides, most texts of Shakespeare will gloss unfamiliar words and phrases for you.

☞ **Prefer watching the plays to reading them.**

All of Shakespeare is available on videotape now. Why not start with the 1993 Kenneth Branagh *Much Ado About Nothing*? Early Modern English didn't stop millions of people from enjoying it. The BBC has a tape series of all the plays of Shakespeare. There are many film versions of *Hamlet*. It's out there if you will only ▮▮▮▮▮▮▮▮▮▮▮▮▮▮▮ **DO IT** .

☞ **Attend some plays.** If you can't find a Shakespeare play, you must live on the South Pole. (Is it true that from there you can walk only north? I've always wondered.) There is nothing like live drama. Them's real people out there doing real stuff.

☞ **Watch-read-watch.** Watch the play, read a text of it, and watch it again (text in lap, to compare). Easiest and cheapest to do with videos. But hey, there's another way in—

☞ **Read the sonnets.** Generally, these are shorter than the plays. They're great. They seem to tell a story—or do they? The speaker has a male friend whom he loves. Many of the sonnets speak of the various stages of this intense friendship. Then we have a woman entering the story, and the speaker falls for her, too—but in a different way. We get a comparison between two different kinds of passion. And some of the poems, especially those in the 140s, are pretty frank.

There are many mysteries surrounding these poems. Shakespeare didn't try to publish them. They were *pirated.* The pirate probably mixed up the original order of the poems, if they had one—meaning *we'll never know what the original order was, or how the story, if there was a story, went!* The sonnets are dedicated to a "Mr. W. H." People have made many guesses as to who W. H. was. No way to tell for sure.

People have gone round the twist for four hundred years about this story. Is the speaker Shakespeare himself? Or just a character he created? (My call: no way to tell.) Is this a comparison between same-sex sex and different- ? (My call: if it is, it's a pretty good one.) Whole forests of trees have fallen over the question of who the male friend was and who the woman.

What we have, DR, is the poems. My goodness, they are good—even when they're trite. (How does he *do* that?)

# Examples of Old Stuff and How to Read It

Most of the Old Stuff is in good translations into contemporary English. See my *Appreciator's Guide* under Chaucer, Dante, Homer, and so forth.

But you want *thee* and *thou*. Okay. Let's select a couple of Old Guys. Here's one: Sir Thomas Wyatt the Elder (1503–1542). Four hundred and fifty years new!

### They Flee from Me

They flee from me, that sometime did me seek,
With naked foot stalking in my chamber.
I have seen them, gentle, tame, and meek,
That now are wild, and do not remember
That sometime they put themselves in danger
To take bread at my hand; and now they range,
Busily seeking with a continual change.

Thankéd be fortune it hath been otherwise,
Twenty times better; but once in special,
In thin array, after a pleasant guise,
When her loose gown from her shoulders did fall,
And she me caught in her arms long and small,
Therewithal sweetly did me kiss
And softly said, "Dear heart, how like you this?"

It was no dream, I lay broad waking.
But all is turned, thorough my gentleness,
Into a strange fashion of forsaking.
And I have leave to go, of her goodness,
And she also to use newfangleness.
But since that I so kindly am servéd,
I fain would know what she hath deservéd.

Now! Do what we have been doing with any poem. Read it aloud. (Modern pronunciation wherever possible, please.) Learn where to put the pauses. Figure out the surprises. Look for the speaker's situation and his attitude toward it.

For Old Stuff, you sometimes need to add some other things:

☞ **Outside information.** Not a stock-market term, but any historical or biographical information that will illuminate the poem. (I'm not giving you any for this one; it doesn't need it.)

☞ **Vocabulary.** There are exactly ten words or phrases you might not recognize here. Most are only slightly different from the words you would use.

*Sometime*, you probably figured out, means *once upon a time*.

*In special* means *especially*.

*Small* means *slender* (sort of nice).

*Therewithal* means *at the same time*.

*Thorough* means *through* and *newfangleness* means *fickleness*. *Kindely* means either *according to her nature* or *in this manner*. *I fain would know* means *I would like to know*.

*In thin array* means they weren't wearing much (it comes off in a second, anyway), and *after a pleasant guise* means they were having some sort of fun masquerade of a certain, er, sort. But you didn't need me to tell you that. As I said, most collections will gloss the words for you. Now fit those suckers back in their lines and work out the meaning.

☞ **Inversions.** Something Old Guys do is twist the grammar of the sentence around in unusual ways. You'll find sentences such as *she me caught in her arms long and small* or phrases such as *did me kiss*—both of which, admit it!, are pretty easy to work out. Inversion can get tricky, of course. Here is a passage from John Milton, an inversion addict. In *Paradise Lost*, Adam is lecturing Eve again:

> O woman, best are all things as the will
> Of God ordained them; his creating hand
> Nothing imperfect or deficient left
> Of all that he created

When you straighten out the inversions, you get

> O woman, all things are best as the will
> Of God ordained them; his creating hand
> Left nothing of all he created
> Imperfect or deficient

which is also pretty, though not poetry.

But don't just translate. Translate, get the meaning, then **let the words snap back into their original order.** As the above shows, the former is Milton, the latter isn't.

And how do you like the Wyatt poem? Learn the (very learnable) vocabulary, work out the (very minor) inversions, and **NOW** read aloud. **DO**  **IT** We'll wait.

Early modern love. The speaker has the normal lover's problem: betrayal. Not extra=original, even in 1530—but he gives it quite a kick. Yes, it's, X-rated. But sweetly—one of, the sweetest embraces in poetry. "Dear heart, how like you this?" Very much, ma'am, thank you. And them small arms. Sometimes it's too good to be true—or, in this case, too true to be good.

## One More Old Guy

Here is a poem by Robert Herrick (1591–1674). Look it over, notice the surprises and highlights, and then read it aloud.

### To the Virgins, to Make Much of Time

Gather ye rosebuds while ye may,
  Old time is still a-flying;
And this same flower that smiles today
  Tomorrow will be dying.

The glorious lamp of heaven, the sun,
  The higher he's a-getting,
The sooner will his race be run,
  And nearer he's to setting.

That age is best which is the first,
  When youth and blood are warmer;
But being spent, the worse, and worst
  Times still succeed the former.

Then be not coy, but use your time,
  And while ye may, go marry;
For having lost but once your prime,
  You may forever tarry.

The word *still* means *always* or *all the time*. And words like *coy* (hard to get) and *tarry* (wait around) you can figure out. Once you are past your prime, baby, you might as well wait around forever. That's right, DR. Folks were thinking about how short their time was three and a half centuries ago.

And few people have said it as well as Herrick.

That is what's great about the Old Guys. And the Old Gals. They said it well, which is why they're still saying it to us. Herrick has a good point, you must admit. If you spend your youth being shy about life, one day you'll turn around and—be a shy old-timer.

 ## Getting Professional Help

Poet General's Warning: **Professional Guidance Is Advised for Some of the Old Stuff.** You deserve your fate if you get a volume of Chaucer, sit down, start reading

> Whan that Aprille with his shoures soote
> The droughte of Marche hath perced to the roote

and expect to get it all. Literature courses exist to guide people through the Old Stuff. A good teacher will light up the Bible, Homer, Vergil, and Milton—not to mention more recent poets! Professional guides are hired to guide. If you want to know Dante—really know him—get professional help.

And once the class is *over*, first thing you do, *read it all again for yourself.*

That is so important my head falls off.

*Literature classes begin the moment after the last class.* That is when it's up to you to go back, open the book, stand up, and **DO** **IT** your own self.

That's when the great old poetry
   starts getting into
 the weave of your life.
It will, too.

# Chapter Five:
# ʃixty-ʃix poetʃ: AN Appreciator'ʃ guide

*Can we get a few things straight here?*

This is **not** the *K-Tel Sixty-Six Greatest Poets of All Time*. This is **not** the *E-Z Shortcut Thru World Poetry*.

**This is a list** of sixty-six poets from different times and places **whose work has something you might like.** I've arranged everyone in alphabetical order. Problems? Questions? Anyone's brain hurt yet? Use this recklessly, casually, read this from front to back, back to front, in threesomes, whatever you want to do. But **DO IT**.

**Features:** Next to the name of each poet, I give a brief idea of his or her life. Then you will find a section called **Like This**. That's an order. **Like This** suggests things to like, things to look for, reasons to sample this poet. **Like This** is followed by **Get This**, a list of books to start with. **Get This** is followed by **And How About**, which lists other poets you might like if you liked this one. (Note: Not all the poets in **And How About** are listed in my sixty-six—if you want to read poets in **And How About**, you have to **DO IT**.

If I think you ought to take a course to get the most out of this poet's work, you will see this: **PGR!!** That stands for **Professional Guidance Recommended!!** *The Waste Land* by T. S. Eliot is a wonderful, harrowing poem—but should it be *the first thing you try?* Here we are, in our first class meeting in Car Mechanics. For your homework, put together this Ferrari!

No way. Start with other things by T. S., and if you get the taste, *The Waste Land* will be there, waiting patiently.

And by the way, why not just start with a few **anthologies**, to let your fingers do the walking? Anthologies are great. The word *anthology* means a "collection of flowers"—use *that* at your next cocktail party. If you want to like poetry, I can't think of a better starting place. You can find anthologies of all kinds. Walk into any good bookstore—or any library. That's how I started. Here is a very brief list of anthologies, just to suggest the range:

*Against Forgetting.* Edited by Carolyn Forché. New York: Norton, 1993. She has brought together poems of conscience, witness, remembrance, and political protest from all over the world. Her book reminds us that writing poetry is often an act of courage and hope, a great answer to those who think poetry doesn't "do anything" worthwhile in the world.

*American Indian Poetry.* Edited by George W. Cronyn. New York: Fawcett, 1991. Everyone should own this book, if only to sample the huge range of fine poetry created by the Native American cultures.

*The Book of French Poetry, 1820-1950.* Edited by William Rees. New York: Viking Penguin, 1991. I lack the space to say how marvelous French poetry is. Translation can give you at least some idea.

*A Drifting Boat: An Anthology of Chinese Zen Poetry.* Edited by J. P. Seaton and Dennis Maloney. Fredonia, N.Y.: White Pine Press, 1994. Two reasons to enjoy Chinese poetry: (1) it has greatly influenced American poetry, making poets think and write in refreshing new ways; (2) it's good.

*The Harvard Book of Contemporary American Poetry.* Edited by Helen H. Vendler. Cambridge: Belknap Press, 1985. This book tries to establish a **canon** of the best American poets. Vendler is the single best-known American poetry critic. Her overviews carry a great deal of information and authority.

*The Longman Anthology of Contemporary American Poetry.* Edited by Stuart Friebert and David G. Young. White Plains, N.Y.: Longman, 1989. The selection of poets here differs from that in Vendler's book, suggesting the astonishing variety and productivity of poetry since World War II.

*The Morrow Anthology of Younger American Poets.* Edited by Dave Smith and David Bottoms. New York: Quill, 1985. This book is even more contemporary than the *Longman*. Smith and Bottoms are fine poets and fine selectors.

*The New Oxford Book of American Verse.* Edited by Richard Ellman. New York: Oxford, 1976. This surveys the history of American poetry, from Anne Bradstreet to people writing very recently. Intelligent selections and introductions.

*The Norton Anthology of Modern Poetry.* Edited by Richard Ellman and Robert O'Clair. New York: Norton, 1988. This is the "big blue book" of British and American poetry in this century. Very fine introductions and selections give you a good taste of each poet. Get it and **DO IT.**

*The Norton Anthology of Poetry.* Edited by Herbert Barrows and others. New York: Norton, 1986. This book provides as good a tour as you'll get of poetry in English throughout the centuries.

*Only Companion: Japanese Poems of Love and Longing.* Translated by Sam Hamill. Boston: Shambhala, 1992. This handsome pocketbook is a good starting point for an exploration of Japanese poetry.

*The Pittsburgh Book of Contemporary American Poetry.* Edited by Ed Ochester and Peter Oresick. Pittsburgh: Univ. Press, 1993. The University of Pittsburgh people are champions of authentic poetry that speaks straightforwardly and movingly about real American lives. This book is a great counterpart to Helen Vendler's *Harvard Book* or J. D. McClatchy's *Vintage Book*. You could create a good American library with *Harvard*, *Vintage*, *Pittsburgh*, *Longman*, *Morrow*, and a couple of *Norton*s. These books show the range of what is considered **poetry**.

*Poets of the English Language, Volume 4: Romantic Poets.* Portable Library no. 52. Edited by W. H. Auden and N. H. Pearson. New York: Viking Penguin, 1977. Blake! Coleridge! Wordsworth! Byron! Shelley! Keats! And many more.

*The Vintage Book of Contemporary American Poetry.* Edited by J. D. McClatchy. New York: Vintage, 1990. The idea here is to give you the greatest number of great contemporary (since Hiroshima) American poets—like the *Harvard Book* but from a slightly different angle.

*Women Romantic Poets.* Edited by Jennifer Breen. London: J. M. Dent, 1992. They were fine poets too, a very well-kept secret. If you're going to buy The Portable Library *Romantic Poets*, why not get this one?

*Working Classics: Poems on Industrial Life.* Edited by Peter Oresick and Nicholas Coles. Urbana, Ill: Univ. Press, 1990. Poems about work, many of them by working people. These are snapshots of reality, time capsules. If you want to learn about the lives of other people, get this book and **DO IT.**

**I'll stop here.** You can get anthologies of poetry in almost any language (Russian, Spanish, German), any period (the Greeks, the Romans, the Middle Ages, the Renaissance), any continent (Africa, South America . . . well, okay, not Antarctica). Start collecting your own flower collections.

Back to our sixty-six poets . . .

 Prices for paperbacks start at $1.00 (in the wonderful Dover Thrift Edition poetry series), and they tend to range between $9.00 and $15.00, though many of the books listed below are cheaper than $10.00. They're less at used book stores—and, again, free at libraries.

At the back is a list of enjoyable poets writing right now, this very moment (think of the thousands of poets writing right now! it's enough to melt your computer), along with a list of journals you can find/read/subscribe to. And if you're not set after that— well, I give up. I just do.

Yes, my bias is toward poets writing in English and toward recent poets. Some of The Heavyweights are here. All the time people ask me, "What's so great about T. S. Eliot? Why should I read Emily Dickinson? What is there to *like* in Homer?"

Well, here you'll find out.

If poets you like aren't in here, it **does not** mean I don't recommend them. I could have put in hundreds more. This *Guide* is just to whet your pleasure centers. Hey—send me your suggestions! Maybe we'll put them in the next edition. (If you do, tell me **what there is to like about their poetry**. That will save me having to make something up.)

## I.Q. What if I don't recognize these people? What if I never heard of 'em?

Okay. Suppose you're at some friends' house, they're cooking you dinner, and they come in with a huge steaming platter of—of *what?* "What's the name of this dish?" you ask. "Forkipselato na Xhosuzzma," they reply. My God! Food Unknown! But now you have to eat it. And you **DO** 🏃 **IT** .

It goes in your mouth.

And it is lovely.

Your whole body and brain change forever. Life is better now. You will tell others about Forkipselato na Xhosuzzma. You will cook it yourself and delight as, thanks to you, others discover it. You will drive cooks and waiters nuts all over the world demanding it.

Very likely there is something—sixty-six things—in the following pages at *least* as good as Forkipselato na Xhosuzzma. (By the way, it's great. You should try it.)

## I.Q. What if I try some and don't like it?

It could happen. If Keats doesn't peel your grape, sample Ovid. If he doesn't stir your yogurt, try Adrienne Rich. If she doesn't lacquer your bannister, there's always Lorca. The world of poetry is a giant supermarket with long aisles and jammed shelves. Start wheeling your cart.

This is, after all, *An Appreciator's Guide*. You want to enjoy yourself? Here are sixy-six ways how.

You should be excited.

Imagine: All this good stuff, just waiting for you.

BUT . . . and there's a big BUT . . . this *Appreciator's Guide* is just a directional arrow. To read these folks, you must actually *do* something! 

# Arise! & **DO** 🏃 **IT**

Put on your Saran Wrap and sun hat! And get thee to the library or the bookstore!

I even tell you what books to get! (*Is this man doing it all for us or what?*) If they don't got 'em, they can order 'em.

True, your life will be in ruins for a few weeks until the books come in. Meanwhile you can distract yourself with minor matters like insurance premiums, smoke detectors, and landscaping.

Once you have the book . . . *Do it, baby*. Sit down and read. Stand up and read. Select a place in the house where you will come upon your little books. When you come upon them, read them.

Everything depends on you.

No pressure here!

Remember: Forkipselato na Xhosuzzma.

Wonderful things unguessed lie in wait.

Do it, baby.

### Akhmatova, Anna (1889-1966)

She was famous as a lyrical, personal poet before the 1917 Russian Revolution derailed her career. From 1922 to about 1940, the Stalinist regime forbade her to publish. She had a brief comeback as a writer of patriotic poetry in the 1940s, but again the government put down its curtain, which was not really raised until the late 1950s.

**Like This**: Here is one courageous woman with bold poems about identity and history. She appreciates life, its intense little moments: "The crow flying with its grating cry, **/** And down the receding path, the curve of an archway." All residents of this century should read her poems about war, womanhood, and history.

**Get This**: *Selected Poems*. Translated by D. M. Thomas. New York: Viking Penguin, 1989; *Poem without a Hero and Other Poems*. Translated by Lenore Mahew and William McNaughton. Oberlin, Ohio: Oberlin College Press, 1989.

**And How About** H.D., Stéphane Mallarmé, Osip Mandelstam, Wilfred Owen, Arthur Rimbaud, Sappho, Marina Tsvetayeva, Paul Verlaine, Yevgeny Yevtushenko?

## Ammons, A. R. (1926 - )

His theme, especially lately, is the interconnectedness of every-thing. In a single poem, he can veer from scientific language to slang—and then to philosophical meditations on the nature of life.

**Like This**: His combination of offhandedness and sudden flashes of scientific exactitude. He really is exploring the way to think now about our lives in this universe. Try these lines:

> when you consider
> that air or vacuum, snow or shale, squid or wolf, rose or
> lichen,
> each is accepted into as much light as it will take, then
> the heart moves roomier, the man stands and looks about, the
>
> leaf does not increase itself above the grass, and the dark
> work of the deepest cells is of a tune with May bushes
> and fear lit by the breadth of such calmly turns to praise.
> ("The City Limits")

 I really like "Each is accepted into as much light as it will take."

**BINGO!**

 Ammons does much praising, much wondering. Read his poems "He Held Radical Light" and "Corsons Inlet." He also has a long poem titled *Garbage*, a marvelous ricochet through the universe.

**Get This**: *Garbage: A Poem*. New York: Norton, 1994; *Really Short Poems of A. R. Ammons*. New York: Norton, 1991; *The Selected Poems*. New York, Norton: 1987.

**And How About** Ben Belitt, Amy Clampitt, Albert Goldbarth, Pattiann Rogers, Gary Snyder, Gerald Stern, Walt Whitman?

## Auden, W. H. (1907-1973)

He's on many people's Century's Best list. Schoolteacher, jour-nalist, freelance writer, political commentator, and world traveler, he witnessed the horrors of the Spanish Civil War, the Sino-

Japanese War, and World War Two. In 1939 he moved to America from England, and he became an American citizen in 1946. In his last fifteen years he moved among England, Austria, and New York.

**Like This**: He is playful and serious at the same time. Few of his poems are without irony, few, no matter how frisky, without a serious point to make. Auden tried all sorts of verse forms. He felt that poetry had a political and moral duty to fulfill, and he acted as an eyewitness to the middle of the twentieth century:

> In the nightmare of the dark
> All the dogs of Europe bark,
> And the living nations wait,
> Each sequestered in its hate
> > ("In Memory of W. B. Yeats")

Powerful. But so is his tender, often ironic poetry of love:

> Lay your sleeping head, my love,
> Human on my faithless arm
> > ("Lullaby")

He is a master satirist, a poet with a sense of humor, and a singer of modern life, betrayal, politics, and religious experience. PGR!! Guidance may be needed for some of his more learned poems—but you can flip through a collected Auden and find many immediately appealing ones. Read him aloud. He has the ring of the wise and lasting. Start with "The Musée des Beaux Arts."

**Get This**: *Collected Poems*. New York: Random House, 1991; *The English Auden*. Edited by Edward Mendelson. Winchester, Mass.: Faber and Faber, 1988.

**And How About** T. S. Eliot, Louis MacNeice, Edwin Muir, Peter Porter, Muriel Rukeyser, Stephen Spender, W. B. Yeats?

## Baraka, Amiri Imamu [formerly LeRoi Jones]
(1934 - )
Poet, playwright, and political force, he is one of today's most distinguished African American literary figures. His poetry, good from the beginning, took on a strong political voice with the Civil

Rights Movement and the increasing self-awareness of the African American community.

**Like This**: He writes an energetic, associational, aggressive poetry. His themes include love, politics, blackness, and popular culture (I like his poems about radio and music). You might find his punctuation and line breaks, shall we say, challenging—but the idea, as always, is to read him aloud.

> & Love is an evil word.
> Turn it backwards/see, what I mean?
> An evol word. & besides
> Who understands it?
> I certainly wouldn't like to go out on that kind of limb.
>
> ("In Memory of Radio")

This is performance poetry that hits you in ways you're never ready for.

**Get This**: *LeRoi Jones—Amiri Baraka Reader*. Edited by William J. Harris. New York: Thunder's Mouth, 1991. He's in most good anthologies of modern American poetry.

**And How About** John Berryman, Lucille Clifton, Allen Ginsberg, Nikki Giovanni, Ntozake Shange, Walt Whitman, William Carlos Williams?

## Bashō [Matsuo Munefusa] (1644 -1694)

Perhaps the most famous of Japanese haiku writers. His simple, powerful style has influenced poets throughout the world.

**Like This**: The profound quietness of his poems. They are built on instants of understanding. You'll find yourself smiling and nodding. They can also connect experiences in startling ways.

> What a loss is here:
> Beneath the warrior's splendid helmet
> A chirping cricket.
>
> (Translated by Earl Miner)

The ultimate in portable poetry, Bashō's words live at the quiet heart of experience.

**Get This**: *Backroads to Far Towns*. Translated by Cid Corman and Kamaike Susumu. Fredonia, N.Y.: White Pine Press, 1986; *Little Enough: Forty-Nine Haiku*. Translated by Cid Corman. Frankfort, Ky.: Gnomon Press, 1991; *On Love and Barley*. Translated by Lucien Stryk. New York: Viking Penguin, 1986.

**And How About** Wendell Berry, John Brandi, Adelaide Crapsey, Ezra Pound, Vikram Seth, Gary Snyder, and Chinese and Japanese poetry, of which there are many fine anthologies?

## Baudelaire, Charles (1821-1867)

In many people's minds he is the model of the dissipated French poet: sickly, languid, smoking hashish in some bordello in the Latin Quarter of Paris. He wrote original and penetrating poetry that hit the literary world like a shock wave.

**Like This**: His poetry is melancholy and sensuous, with dark anxieties behind the lines. Baudelaire, who knew about life, wrote some of the frankest poems you will find about pleasure and moral degradation. He was also a passionate lover of women, and his love poetry is original, disarming, and thoroughly convincing.

> I adore you like the vaulted archways of night,
> O vase of sadness, silent woman;
> All the more since you flee from me,
> Because you seem, ornament of my nights,
> Mockingly to build up the leagues
> Between my arms and the blue immensities.
>
> I advance to the attack, creep up the battlements,
> Like a choir of worms around a body,
> And I cherish—cruel, implacable beast!—
> Even the coldness that makes you more beautiful.
>> ("I Adore You Like the Vaulted Archways of Night")

There is something slightly repellent in his feverish intensity—but you can't deny its power. (You can see why he liked Edgar Allan Poe!) He is one of the very few poets in whom the sense of *smell* is strong, alluring, piercing. Reading him combines a descent into hell and an emergence into a brilliant world of sharp pleasures and sharper truths.

**Get This**: *Selected Poems*. Edited by Joanna Richardson. New York: Viking Penguin, 1975.

**And How About** Hart Crane, T. S. Eliot, Stéphane Mallarmé, Gérard de Nerval, Edgar Allan Poe, Ezra Pound, Rainer Maria Rilke, Arthur Rimbaud, Paul Verlaine?

## Berry, Wendell (1934 - )

He doubles as a college professor and a farmer on seventy-five acres in Kentucky. I want his job(s). God knows when he has time to write his poetry, but I'm glad he does.

**Like This**: He is one of our quiet masters. His poems on family, love, farming, nature, war, and time are very clear, precise, to the point. He has written some fine plays in that same clear, clean poetry. Keep one of his books around the house; pick him up, open almost anywhere, and within seconds something real and bracing and sweet will happen to you.

**Get This**: *Collected Poems, 1957-1982*. New York: Farrar, Straus and Giroux, 1987; *Entries: Poems*. New York: Pantheon, 1994; *Farming: A Hand Book*. New York: Harcourt Brace, 1971.

**And How About** Emily Dickinson, Robert Frost, Maxine Kumin, Les Murray, Vikram Seth, Timothy Steele?

## Bishop, Elizabeth (1911-1979)

She appears on many people's Century's Best list.

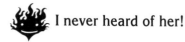 I never heard of her!

Well, DR, now you have. She was born in Massachusetts but lived an uprooted, peripatetic life in the United States, Brazil, and elsewhere.

**Like This**: She is two poets in one. She can be quiet, reticent, ironic, often improvisational. In this key, she is a poet who can teach you about life.

> The art of losing isn't hard to master;
> so many things seem filled with the intent
> to be lost that their loss is no disaster.
>
> *("One Art")*

I've never recovered from reading that first line.

She can also hit us with flashes of tremendously vivid imagery. Maybe you read "The Man-Moth" or "The Fish" in high school. Those poems show how she can make you see, feel, hear, and taste the image in front of you.                **DO IT**

> He hung a grunting weight
> battered and venerable
> and homely. Here and there
> his brown skin hung in strips
> like ancient wallpaper
> ("The Fish")

She sneaks up on you—sometimes quietly, sometimes vividly, most of the time both. **CAUTION**: it's easy to think her a nice, quiet poet, but as the clips above show, her whispers are sticks of **TNT.**

**Get This**: *Complete Poems*: *1927-1979*. New York: Farrar, Straus and Giroux, 1984; *Geography III*. New York: Farrar, Straus and Giroux, 1976.

**And How About** Louise Bogan, Robert Lowell, Marianne Moore, Adrienne Rich, Theodore Roethke, Muriel Rukeyser?

## Blake, William (1757-1827)

Many of us know "The Lamb" and "The Tyger," but if you want a true head-clearing—little poems that take up permanent residence in your frontal lobes—get a copy of *Songs of Innocence and Experience* and read it front to back. There are many editions out there. Get one with the original illustrations, also by Blake.

**Like This**: Blake was far ahead of his time—or any other time. This Englishman had a bold, mystical, idiosyncratic vision. He hated kings, social inequality, cruelty, and oppression. Imagination was everything. Many of his poems are in very simple language—

### The Sick Rose

O Rose, thou art sick.
The invisible worm
That flies in the night
In the howling storm

Has found out thy bed
Of crimson joy,
And his dark secret love
Doth thy life destroy.

—but these simple poems pack a punch.

 **A pocket-sized nightmare.**

Good one, DR. There is a dark wildness to Blake—but there is also tenderness, toward children, lambs, good people, and the Divine. Here is a man who felt deeply with everything he had.

**Get This**: *Selected Poems*. Edited by P. H. Butter. Boston: Tuttle, 1993; *Songs of Innocence and Songs of Experience*. New York: Dover, 1992.

**And How About** Anna Akhmatova; W. H. Auden; George Gordon, Lord Byron; Johann Wolfgang von Goethe; John Keats; Friedrich von Schiller; Percy Bysshe Shelley; William Wordsworth; W. B. Yeats?

## Browning, Robert (1812 - 1889)

He had one of the most famous, happiest love affairs in history with Elizabeth Barrett, who became his wife and lifelong love. They eloped to Italy and lived there until her death. She was the more famous, more beloved poet (and you should read her, too), but after her death, he came into a period of great creativity and popularity.

**Like This**: If you want stories, if you want characters, if you want a voice speaking to you with optimism, confidence, and energy, pick up some of Browning's poems. His favorite form is the **_dramatic monologue_**, in which someone—often some obscure person from history—speaks directly to us in a personal, straightforward way. Many are like small novels. Often you have to be a detective and piece together the truth. Start with "My Last Duchess." Read it and figure it out.

He became a superb poet of description—his landscapes, his cities, his scenes are very vivid. Here is a well-known passage from "Meeting at Night":

> I gain the cove with pushing prow,
> And quench its speed i' the slushy sand. . . .
>
> Then a mile of warm sea-scented beach;
> Three fields to cross till a farm appears;
> A tap at the pane, the quick sharp scratch
> And blue spurt of a lighted match,
> And a voice less loud, through its joys and fears,
> Than the two hearts beating each to each!

Browning in a nutshell. A breathless miniature story. And can you hear his hearty music? Say "And quench its speed i' the slushy sand."

Say it five times fast. I recommend his book *Men and Women*— Browning at the height. Listen to his people talk.

**Get This**: *The Essential Browning*. New York: Galahad, 1992; *Men and Women: And Other Poems*. Edited by J. W. Harper. Boston: Tuttle, 1993.

**And How About** W. H. Auden; Elizabeth Barrett Browning; George Gordon, Lord Byron; T. S. Eliot; Robert Frost; Richard Howard; Edgar Lee Masters; Peter Porter; Ezra Pound; Edwin Arlington Robinson; Alfred, Lord Tennyson; William Wordsworth?

## Byron [George Gordon, Lord Byron] (1788-1824)

This man's life is the stuff of movies. Along with Shelley, Keats, Beethoven, Goethe, Hugo, and Wordsworth, he helped invent the Romantic era. One of the great figures in world literature, he was born wealthy, lived large, slept with half of Europe, and backed up his liberal politics by joining in the Greek war for independence. Bad career move. He died of a fever near Missolonghi, Greece.

**Like This**: The word *Byronic* still means "tempestuous, lusty, passionate, self-involved." Byron himself was not always like this—but he helped create that Romantic character in his first big poem, *Childe Harold's Pilgrimage*, a Matterhorn of vast, dark energy. He was also a fine lyric poet, an appreciator of love and beauty:

> She walks in Beauty, like the night
>   Of cloudless climes and starry skies;
> And all that's best of dark and bright
>   Meet in her aspect and her eyes
>                           ("She Walks in Beauty")

Start with his lyric poems, which you can find almost anywhere. But if you want the best Byron, you should dip into *Don Juan* (pronounced Don JOO-an), a huge comic masterpiece about an oddly innocent fellow who keeps getting into trouble (romantic, philosophical, and otherwise). Byron's true talent, in the end, was comic verse. *Don Juan* is life itself, DR, along with delightfully immoral reflections and some amazing rhyming: **DO ☞ IT**

> But—Oh! ye lords of ladies intellectual,
> Inform us truly, have they not henpecked you all?

So read the lyrics, *Don Juan*, and maybe, with Beethoven booming in the background, *Childe Harold*.

**Get This**: *Selected Poems*. New York: Dover, 1993; *Don Juan*. Edited by Leslie A. Marchand. Boston: Houghton Mifflin, 1972.

**And How About** Samuel Taylor Coleridge, Johann Wolfgang von Goethe, John Keats, Aleksandr Pushkin, Friedrich von Schiller, Percy Bysshe Shelley, William Wordsworth?


## Catullus, Gaius Valerius (84 - 54 B.C.)

He wrote short, personal poems about love, sex, friendship, and other passions in the generation before Christ. His most famous poems are those he wrote to his beloved Lesbia:

Lesbia, let us live and let us love.
Forget what the strict oldsters say.
Suns can set and rise again,
But for us, when our brief light sets,
night is one perpetual sleep.
Give me a thousand kisses, then a hundred,
Then a second thousand, then another hundred,
Then yet another thousand . . .

I'm getting hot. Before Catullus, Latin was a language in which to count soldiers, cities, and bales of wool, not a language of lyricism. He wasn't the first to write of love in Latin, but he was one of the first to show you could do it well.

**Like This**: His chronicle of the Lesbia affair is convincing and direct. You can feel, across two millennia, a man suffering his way through betrayal. When he is hurt, he tells himself, "Bear up, Catullus, you can handle it," but he can't. His attacks on his enemy Gellius are hilariously smutty. He has beautiful descriptive poetry, and moving poetry on friendship and loss.

**Get This**: *The Poems of Catullus*. Translated by Peter Whigham. New York: Viking Penguin, 1980.

**And How About** e. e. cummings, Dante, John Donne, Thom Gunn, Horace, George Meredith, Ovid, Petrarch, Theodore Roethke, Sappho?

### Chaucer, Geoffrey (1343-1400)

I know very few people who have actually read Chaucer and don't like him. He led quite a life: ambassador, sidekick to the rich and powerful, the equivalent of Head Customs Inspector for England, Justice of the Peace. When did he find the *time* to write all that poetry? He was a practical man who knew life as lived. And does his poetry ever show it! No one—even today—is more focused on the concerns of everyday people.

 But his everyday people lived six hundred years ago! And what about his Olde Englysshe withe ye weirde spellynges that I cannot readde? Please don't make me read him.

I won't. Not in the original. Read him in a modern translation—*then*, with professional guidance, read him in the original. You'll see why graffitists everywhere write, "Chauc rules!"

**Like This**: His amused, humane tolerance for everything human. He is great at creating characters—for example, sexy Alisoun, tricky Nicholas, and the oaf John in "The Miller's Tale." Get a modern translation of *The Canterbury Tales* and flip through. I recommend "The General Prologue," "The Knight's Tale," "The Miller's Tale," "The Wife of Bath's Tale," "The Nun's Priest's Tale," and anything else you like. Chaucer is famous for his sense of humor and for being "dirty," but **donnez-moi un break!** A better word would be *bawdy*—off-color, perhaps, but with a twinkle. I do admire Nicholas's method of saying hi to Alisoun—by grabbing her "haunche-bone." Don't try this at home.

And then there's *Troilus and Criseyde*. When war confronts love, something's got to give. I think his Criseyde is one of the best female characters ever created by a male author; this complex woman wants to love but knows how the world goes. (Chaucer had a good eye for women—not too common, even among the greats.)

**PGR!!** After reading him in translation, read him in the original with a professional guide. His tales translate well—but you don't get the true Chaucer unless you read him in the original. Oh my brothers and sisters,

**DO IT**

**Get This**: *The Canterbury Tales*. Translated by Nevill Coghill. New York: Viking, 1951; *The Canterbury Tales*. Translated by A. Kent Hieatt and Constance B. Hieatt. New York: Bantam, 1982; *The Canterbury Tales*. Edited and translated by David Wright. New York: Oxford Univ. Press, 1986; *Troilus and Criseyde*. Translated by Nevill Coghill. New York: Viking Penguin, 1971.

**And How About** Giovanni Boccaccio, Dante, *Sir Gawain and the Green Knight*—and more Chaucer?

## Coleridge, Samuel Taylor (1772 - 1834)

A teacher once told me that Coleridge was famous for writing ten good poems in his whole life. Well, I'd give my good angel to have written any one of them. Coleridge was the close friend and poetic ally of William Wordsworth, and together they published a little book called *Lyrical Ballads* (1798), which marked a big change in English poetry, pretty much for good.

**Like This**: Go get an anthology of English poetry, look up "Kubla Khan," stand in a room, and read that thing aloud at the top of your voice. Coleridge wanted to capture that first moment of inspiration, and this poem comes pretty close.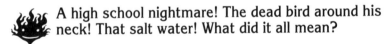

> In Xanadu did Kubla Khan
> A stately pleasure-dome decree:
> Where Alph, the sacred river, ran
> Through caverns measureless to man
>   Down to a sunless sea.

**Yahoo!** What does it all mean? Who cares? Yahoo! This is a bucking, blazing poem about bucking, blazing feelings. It launches a firestorm of senses—and then it breaks off, unfinished. That's Romantic poetry for you.

Coleridge also was interested in the occult, in half-understood ghost tales. These include "The Rime of the Ancient Mariner"—

**A high school nightmare! The dead bird around his neck! That salt water! What did it all mean?**

I don't know. Nobody does. But the tale stays with you. You can't translate the uncanny feeling it gives you. Same for *Christabel*. He was very good at writing about parts of our lives we don't understand very clearly.

And Coleridge was one of the first of the Romantic nature poets. Read "This Lime-Tree Bower My Prison," "Frost at Midnight," or "Dejection: An Ode."

**Get This**: *Poems*. Edited by John Beer. Boston: Tuttle, 1993.

**And How About** George Gordon, Lord Byron; John Keats; Percy Bysshe Shelley?

## cummings, e. e. (1894 - 1962)

because he has few capital letters, or BEc/AuSe H / ewrite SIN oddBALL wayz, people think of him as *the* avant-garde poet. but when you read him, you get love, april, roses, rain, god, sex—the basic menu. and that's fine.

cummings was an ambulance driver in the first world war, and a poet, painter, bohemian, lecturer, and much else for the rest of his time.

**Like This**: Surprise! He is actually pretty easy to understand. What's so hard about this?:

nine birds(rising

through a gold moment)climb:
ing i

-nto
wintry
twi-

light
(alltogether a
manying
one

-ness)nine
souls
only alive with a single mys-

tery(liftingly
caught upon falling)silent!

ly living the dying of glory

His shenanigans increase the delight of reading him. No one, but no one, can get the effects he can get. Many are the trenchant lines ("goodby Betty, don't remember me" or "a salesman is an it that stinks Excuse" or "a politician is an arse upon **/** which everyone has sat except a man"). At least four of his poems—"in Just-," "Buffalo Bill's," "anyone lived in a pretty how town," and "my father moved through dooms of love"—are among the best of the century.

**Get This**: *Selected Poems: E. E. Cummings*. With introduction and commentary by Richard S. Kennedy. New York: Liveright, 1994.

**And How About** Ted Berrigan, Catullus, Gregory Corso, Don Marquis, Gertrude Stein?

**Dante [Alighieri]** (1265 - 1321)

Along with Petrarch and Boccaccio, Dante stands as one of the beginnings, and one of the high points, of Italian literature. He helped invent personal love poems, and he pretty much cornered the market on poems about heaven and hell.

**Like This**: What he was after, like many of us, was The Ultimate. He fell in love with this Beatrice woman on a bridge one day, and after that, life just burned with a godlike intensity. The Ultimate is what we get with Dante—whether we're falling in love, exploring the depths, or ascending to beatific union with the Divine.

*La Vita Nuova*, a diary of Dante's love for Beatrice, carefully follows how his viewpoint and feelings change after he realizes his love for her. It changed the way people wrote about love, according to DuJuan Shchvsdok of Sweltering Swale, Florida.

*The Divine Comedy* is a three-part tour of Hell, Purgatory, and Paradise, bringing all the history, science, and poetry Dante knew (and he knew a great deal) into the tour. **PGR!!**—even though you can appreciate much of this poem on your own, there's a great deal of history, literature, and local politics in it (he puts a few of his enemies in the Big Oven). Once we get to Paradise, there is Beatrice. Love for her turns out to be the way to God. In Canto XXIII of *Paradiso* we finally get to look on the Divine:

> Oh overflowing grace, because of which I dared
> to fix my glance on the Eternal Light
> so long my vision was nearly consumed—
> In Its depths I saw gathered up,
> bound with love into one volume,
> all the pages scattered throughout the universe

**BINGO! You bet!** You have to admire the reach—and the grasp.

**Get This**: *The Inferno of Dante: A New Verse Translation*. Translated by Robert Pinsky. New York: Farrar, Straus and Giroux, 1994; *La Vita Nuova*. Edited by Mark Musa. New York: Oxford Univ. Press, 1992; *The Portable Dante*. Translated and edited by Mark Musa. New York: Viking Penguin, 1993.

**And How About** Giovanni Boccaccio, Geoffrey Chaucer, John Donne, T. S. Eliot, Gerard Manley Hopkins, John Milton, Octavio Paz, Petrarch, Rainer Maria Rilke?

## Dickinson, Emily (1830 - 1886)

Spinster-recluse living in Amherst, Massachusetts. Only a couple of poems published during her lifetime—but then the poems are discovered and published, and everyone falls down. She and Whitman are in a first-place tie, so to speak, for the honor of being America's first really great poet—according to Sophonisba La Frontiere of Single Rut, South Dakota.

**Like This**: Her poems are easy to read, short, and immediate. Her themes are loneliness, joy, love, death, heaven. And so forth. She is very original. Some people think she was crazy. I have no idea what she was. All I know is, she wrote shocking stuff, happy, witty, bitter, ironic, ambiguous. And explosive. Anyone who can write

> My Life had stood—a Loaded Gun—
> In Corners—till a Day
> The Owner passed—identified—
> And carried Me away—

is not fooling around.

Open the book to any page and an instant later, feel sheer perplexed amazement. An American female unique.

**Get This**: She is everywhere, in most good anthologies of American poetry. There is an excellent selection, for example, in *The Norton Anthology of Literature by Women*: *The Tradition in English*. Edited by Sandra M. Gilbert and Susan Gubar. New York: Norton, 1985. Also, there is *Selected Poems*. New York: Tom Doherty Assoc., 1993.

**And How About** John Berryman, Robert Frost, Robert Lowell, Sylvia Plath, Adrienne Rich, May Sarton, Anne Sexton?

## Donne, John (1572 - 1631)

Roughly contemporary with Shakespeare, he made some very bad career moves in marriage and religion. Eventually he converted to the Church of England and became Dean of St. Paul's Church. You could say that Donne, as a poet, has happened twice: once during and just after his lifetime, and again in the twentieth century, when he was rediscovered.

**Like This**: He uses his bold, outrageous imagination to find connections between very dissimilar things. When a man wants to praise the woman he is about to get naked with, he calls her "my America! My new-found-land." Get it? A man leaving his wife for a long journey tells her that their love is like the two legs of a compass—the kind you couldn't draw a circle with back in geometry class.

> Thy soul, the fixed foot, makes no show
>   To move, but doth, if th'other do.
>
> And though it in the center sit,
>   Yet when the other far doth roam,
> It leans and hearkens after it,
>   And grows erect, as that comes home.
>                 ("A Valediction: Forbidding Mourning")

Clever, eh? But more than clever—he thought this idea through and somehow made it work. (How does he *do* that?)

**POET GENERAL'S WARNING**: John Donne is extremely seductive to women. I don't know why (but wish I did). Guess that's why he is one of the most popular of all love poets. But he has more. His *Holy Sonnets* are some of the greatest religious poems in history ("Batter my heart, three-personed God; for you / As yet but knock, breathe, shine, and seek to mend"). He is a challenge to the head and heart. PGR!!—but you can get into many Donne poems without much help.

**Get This**: *The Love Poems of John Donne*. Edited by Charles Faulkes. New York: St. Martin's, 1982; *Selected Poems*. Edited by John Hayward. New York: Viking Penguin, 1986. Donne is in many anthologies.

**And How About** W. H. Auden; Richard Crashaw; T. S. Eliot; Fulke Greville, Lord Brooke; George Herbert; Robert Herrick; Ben Jonson; William Shakespeare; Henry Vaughan?

## Dorn, Ed (1929 - )

He writes about all the things that make up identity—including geology and geography, politics, philosophy, and science.

**Like This**: Ed Dorn's poetry tries to suggest the interconnected totality of all things surrounding us; he likes to play with the way our environment affects our identity and vice versa. His long poem *Gunslinger* stars a postmodern Zen cowboy on a tour of the universe. Gunslinger and the speaker are talking:

> And why do you have a female horse
> Gunslinger? I asked. Don't move
> he replied
> the sun rests deliberately
> on the rim of the sierra.

Gunslinger doesn't want the speaker to "disturb" the sun, which rests in an important way on the horizon. *Gunslinger* is a poem about finding a way to see oneself whole. It's worth a read.

**Get This**: *Gunslinger*. Durham, N.C.: Duke Univ. Press, 1989.

**And How About** Robert Bly, Allen Ginsberg, W. S. Merwin, Charles Olson, Gary Snyder, William Carlos Williams?

## Eliot, T. S. (1888 -1965)

Okay ... here we go ...

The other day, I heard some exasperated person cry out, "Who am I? T. S. *Eliot?*" Eliot has become proverbial for a brainy poet no one understands. That's our loss, DR, although I can see how it happened. He deserves the reputation—but not all the blame.

Born in St. Louis, he was educated at Harvard and the Sorbonne, moved to England, and stayed there. He worked for Lloyd's Bank for a while, and eventually he was able to live as an editor, poet, essayist, and famous person. He won the Nobel Prize for Literature in 1948. When his great poems first appeared, it seemed as if the old ways of writing were dissolving and a new way had arrived. Eliot became a leading figure in modern culture, though he himself became profoundly conservative in his religious and political views.

**Like This**: PGR!! If you want to read *The Waste Land*, if you want to read *Four Quartets*, join a group with a **Fearless Leader** who can shed light on all the learned allusions, spates of foreign languages, and, well, weirdness:

London Bridge is falling down falling down falling down
*Poi s'ascose nel foco che gli affina*
*Quando fiam uti chelidon*—O swallow swallow
*Le Prince d'Aquitaine à la tour abolie*
These fragments I have shored against my ruins
Why then Ile fit you. Hieronymo's mad againe.
(The Waste Land)

 Can I ask a question here? Just one? Is it any wonder that so many people like me, who had to read this stuff in high school, hate it, hate it, *hate* it? This is what gives poetry a bad name. You want to put the book down and run screaming from the room! Okay—you're right—most poetry, you can get at. But this—don't tell me to love this. I won't, and you can't make me.

You're right.

 Oh, come on. I want a fight here!

They shouldn't have made you read this in high school. You need to *know* too much.

 What about you? When you first read this poem, did you understand it?

No. Still don't. But it was one of the most frightening things that ever happened to me. So much of it speaks of hell, of things breaking apart, of cosmic forces, urban life, uncertainty, and fear—I could *feel* my way through.

So?

So don't read Eliot if it makes you hate poetry. Open a book of Robert Frost or Wendell Berry or Emily Dickinson.

**Hear this**, though: Eliot had music. He had a new way to write. And he was afraid of madness and the decline of civilized life. So he had (and still has) much to say. When he writes, in *The Waste Land*, "We think of the key, each in his prison / Thinking of the key, each confirms a prison," he is speaking to our loneliness and our inward-turning isolation.

DR—if you haven't gone away—read a little of "The Love Song of J. Alfred Prufrock" and see whether you feel better.

> And indeed there will be time
> To wonder, "Do I dare?" and, "Do I dare?"
> Time to turn back and descend the stair,
> With a bald spot in the middle of my hair—
> (They will say: "How his hair is growing thin!")
> My morning coat, my collar mounting firmly to the chin,
> My necktie rich and modest, but asserted by a simple pin—
> (They will say: "But how his arms and legs are thin!")
> Do I dare
> Disturb the universe?
> In a minute there is time
> For decisions and revisions which a minute will reverse.

How about those lines, DR?

 I like them. They're true.

Eliot didn't write that much poetry. But when he did write something, it tended to become famous. Besides "Prufrock" and *The Waste Land* you've got "The Hollow Men"—

 Oh, Mother of Bruce! "We are the hollow men"! I could have slaughtered Miss Hrniak for making us read that.

Okay, okay. He also wrote religious poetry, such as *Ash Wednesday*, and he tried to make himself a playwright. My favorite of his poems is *Four Quartets*, a meditation on, among other things, the Divine and human history. PGR!! Like *The Waste Land*, this is not an easy poem. It is sublimely beautiful, though, and glows when read aloud. With T. S., we're on a pretty elevated plane. Even when we're talking about coffee spoons, we're also talking about the direction of history, the plight of the human soul, the moral nature of art, and the presence of God. This is a place populated by Dante, Homer, Milton, Yeats, and the highest aimers. That's a good reason for sampling their work. It's not as though these aren't important questions.

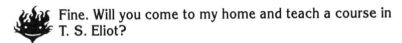 **Fine. Will you come to my home and teach a course in T. S. Eliot?**

Call my agent.

**Get This:** *Collected Poetry, 1909-1962.* New York: Harcourt Brace, 1963; *Selected Poems.* New York: Harcourt Brace, 1967. The man is everywhere.

**And How About** W. H. Auden, Dante, John Donne, H.D., Edwin Muir, Ezra Pound, Laura Riding, Anne Ridler, William Shakespeare, Dylan Thomas, R. S. Thomas, W. B. Yeats?

## Frost, Robert (1874 - 1963)

Born in—surprise—San Francisco, he lived most of his life in New England. His career started late. His indifferent success at poultry farming made him seek a job as a teacher. To be discovered, he had to move to England, where his first two books were published. There followed a distinguished career as a poet, lecturer, and teacher, including four Pulitzer Prizes.

**Like This:** I've always been amazed by the sheer number of *good poems* he wrote. People do know and love them. My sister-in-law has "The Road Not Taken" in a frame on her wall, to remind herself of her own direction. Other folks have framed "Fire and Ice" or "Stopping by Woods on a Snowy Evening."

Many of his poems present New England scenes and people as larger-than-life archetypes of human problems. He writes in colloquial American without either slipping into slang or giving up rhyme and meter. (People talk all the time about doing that, but Frost is almost the only one who actually did it.)

He is a tremendous dramatic poet. Read "Home Burial," "The Death of the Hired Man," "West-Running Brook," or "The Witch of Coös." He has wonderful monologues, too, such as "The Wood-Pile." Good scenes, good characters, very important questions. But he's not telling the story to give you provincial New England—he's talking about our lives and our ways of seeing them.

He was also a philosophical poet, wondering about time, the order of creation, the nature of friendship, and the end of the world. Read "Design," "Birches," "Fire and Ice," "Acquainted with the Night," and "For Once, Then, Something." He does what we want poets to do: think aloud about the Big Questions. He is also a fine, wry love poet ("Love at the lips was touch **/** As sweet as I could bear"), another whose lines ring in the mind.

Get his *Collected Poems* and perch that sucker on your shelf. It will be a fine companion.

**Get This**: *The Poetry of Robert Frost: The Collected Poems, Complete and Unabridged*. New York: Henry Holt, 1975; *The Road Not Taken and Other Poems*. New York: Dover, 1993; *Selected Poems*. New York: Random House, 1992. Huge helpings of Frost appear in most anthologies of American poetry.

**And How About** Wendell Berry, Emily Dickinson, Maxine Kumin, Edgar Lee Masters, Edwin Arlington Robinson, Walt Whitman?

## García Lorca, Federico (1899 - 1936)

He's one of the best-known Spanish poets of this century, famous for his poems about Andalusia (his native province in Spain), gypsies, and bullfighting. He was killed in Granada under mysterious circumstances at the beginning of the Spanish Civil War.

**Like This**: He's very Spanish, very dreamlike, yet another poet who was looking for some alternative to the fakery of industrialized urban culture. Maybe that's why he was drawn to the myths and passions of the gypsies. Read his poems about bullfighting, especially "Lament for the Death of a Bullfighter." Sooner or later, the bullfighter makes a bad career move.     **DO** 🏃 **IT**

> Neither the bull nor the fig tree knows you—
> Not the horses, not the ants of your house.
> Neither the child nor the afternoon knows you
> Because you have died forever.

He translates beautifully into English. He's simple enough so that Spanish-speaking schoolkids everywhere know his poems—and adult enough so that, once you read him, you're not likely to forget him.

Lorca was also a fine playwright. Read *Blood Wedding* or *The House of Bernarda Alba*. A BBC version of the latter is available on videotape. Well worth watching.

**Get This:** *Selected Poems.* Edited by Donald M. Allen. New York: New Directions, 1962; *Selected Poems.* [English and Spanish] Edited by Christopher Maurer. New York: Farrar, Straus and Giroux, 1993.

**And How About** Robert Frost, Juan Ramón Jiménez, Hugh MacDiarmid, Pablo Neruda, César Vallejo?

## Gilgamesh (3000 - 2000 B.C.)

You could call this the first poem. King Gilgamesh, a real person, ruled over Uruk, one of the first-ever cities in history. A group of Sumerian poems record his adventures and battles.

**Like This:** The two best-known episodes concern a Great Flood (sound familiar?) and Gilgamesh's journey to the land of the dead to bring back his friend, the beast/man Enkidu. We're really reaching back to the beginning of things with *Gilgamesh*, but it speaks about the very issues that haunt us still: the purpose of living, our relations with the land, with other living beings, with the gods. Five thousand years—almost the entire span of civilized life—haven't dimmed the force or clarity of these stories.

**Get This:** *Gilgamesh: A New Rendering in English Verse.* Translated by David Ferry. New York: Farrar, Straus and Giroux, 1992; *Gilgamesh: A Verse Narrative.* Translated by Herbert Mason. New York: New American Library/Dutton, 1972. (Herbert Mason's rendering of the Enkidu tale, written after Mason's own experience of loss, is very moving.)

**And How About** Dante, The Book of Genesis, Hesiod, Homer, Lucretius, Vergil?

## Goldbarth, Albert (1948 - )

If it's variety you want, read him. He has written a ton of poetry, and he writes about everything in as many ways as he can think of. His aim seems to be to tackle the everything-at-once of modern life with an anything-at-all-times kind of poetry. Slang sits next to journalese next to academic language; the beautiful, the appalling, and the what-is-it? go hand in hand.

**Like This**: His energy. His many styles. His range of emotion, from passion to enthusiasm to perplexity. Many of his poems read like essays, and they wander into some interesting places. Language tends to explode all over the place.

> The wind at my body is wild
> animals licking for salt. I've set a
> sheet of galleys down and come outside for these
> rough tongues! The wind in the monstrous condor
> flappings of my banana tree leaves,
> the wind in the twiddling back grasses.
> No ant egg is free.
>                              ("A Theory of Wind")

One of the most energetic poets going. You will recognize many of the worlds Goldbarth conjures up: they add up to the one you're living in.

**Get This**: *Arts and Sciences*. Princeton: Ontario Review, 1986; *Original Light*: *New and Selected Poems, 1973-1983*. Princeton: Ontario Review, 1983; *Popular Culture*. Columbus, Oh.: Ohio State Univ. Press, 1990.

**And How About** A. R. Ammons, Amy Clampitt, Lawrence Ferlinghetti, Allen Ginsberg, Robert Pinsky, Gerald Stern, Walt Whitman?

## Hall, Donald (1928 - )

He is the kind who gives poetry a good name. Educated at Harvard, Oxford, and Stanford, among other places, he has been writing for more than four decades now. For many years, he and his wife, the poet Jane Kenyon (read her poetry too), lived in a farmhouse in New Hampshire and worked at writing the best poetry they could.

**Like This**: Though a trifle brainy sometimes, he writes for people to read him. I enjoy his sense of humor and his wide range of topics. He has the best poem about cheese I have read.

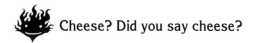 **Cheese? Did you say cheese?**

Yes, DR. When the chips are down and you need that poem on cheese and fast, now you know where to go. Here are a few lines in which he praises

> dear dense cheeses, Cheddars and harsh
> Lancashires; Gorgonzola with its magnanimous manner;
> the clipped speech of Roquefort; and a head of Stilton
> that speaks in a sensuous riddling tongue like Druids.
> ("O Cheese")

**Break out the vino and let's have a party!**

You have to like someone who will tackle an assignment like "Write a poem about cheese."

I like the poems in which he explores some aspect of his own life, trying to get to the truth of the matter, which he often does. He has written very well on sickness, comfort, time, and baseball. He has done some fine children's verse, too.

**Get This:** *Old and New Poems.* New York: Ticknor and Fields, 1990. Donald Hall appears in most good anthologies of recent American poetry.

**And How About** Randall Jarrell, Galway Kinnell, Marianne Moore, Theodore Roethke, Karl Shapiro?

## H.D. (1886 - 1961)

Her name was actually Hilda Doolittle. She was born in Bethlehem, Pennsylvania, and went to Bryn Mawr, only to fall in love with the poet Ezra Pound and follow him (sort of) to England. She lived (without him) in England and Switzerland from then on.

**Like This:** When young, she wrote spare, stripped, achingly vivid poems that knock us in the soul with their hard imagery.

### Heat

O wind, rend open the heat,
cut apart the heat,
rend it to tatters.

Fruit cannot drop
through this thick air—
fruit cannot fall into heat
that presses up and blunts
the points of pears
and rounds the grapes.

Cut the heat—
plough through it,
turning it on either side
of your path.

**BINGO!** **Uh-huh!** There is a perfectness to that, an immediate, real energy. Many people saw these poems when they first came out, and many were influenced by them.

Later, she wrote longer, more mystical, more learned poetry. I especially like her narrative poem *The Walls Do Not Fall*.

**Get This:** *Selected Poems.* Introduction by Louis L. Martz. New York: New Directions, 1988. She is in most anthologies of modern poetry.

**And How About** Robert Duncan, T. S. Eliot, F. S. Flint, Denise Levertov, Marianne Moore, Sylvia Plath, Ezra Pound, William Carlos Williams?

## Heaney, Seamus (1939- )

He is an Irish poet who writes of his youth, Ireland, history, anthropology (Neolithic people dug up from bogs), and much else.

**Like This:** His music. What an ear he has! He's moving, witty, sometimes violent. Sometimes PGR*!*—but everyone should be able to find a Heaney poem to like (see the excerpt from "Death of a Naturalist," page 29).

**Get This:** *Selected Poems 1966-1987.* New York: Farrar, Straus and Giroux, 1991.

**And How About** Austin Clarke, Thomas Hardy, Ted Hughes, Philip Larkin, Paul Muldoon?

# Hecht, Anthony (1923 - )

His subject is our century. He has very moving poems on the Holocaust, on ways of living a balanced, reasonably happy life in the din of the present age.

**Like This**: Here is someone whose poetry rhymes much of the time. Its formality is a comfort to many readers. Can he turn a verse or what? And yet he is not old-fashioned. He is talking about our moment, about history. His poems of war and cruelty are breathtaking. A Polish man is forced to bury two Jews alive, is shot in the belly, and bleeds to death:    **DO IT**

> No prayers or incense rose up in those hours
> Which grew to be years, and every day came mute
> Ghosts from the ovens, sifting through crisp air,
> And settled upon his eyes in a black soot.
> ("More Light! More Light!")

Aware of the barely curbed violence within most people, he still has humor. He is a poet living right now and trying to make sense of it. Hecht is one of our best.

**Get This**: *Collected Earlier Poems*. New York: Knopf, 1990; *The Venetian Vespers*. New York: Macmillan, 1979.

**And How About** Donald Davie, Dana Gioia, Donald Hall, John Hollander, Randall Jarrell, Robert Lowell, Robert Pinsky, Gjertrud Schnackenberg?

# Homer (about 9th century B.C.)

You're blind and you live on this island. So what do you do? Start Western culture, that's what. Some people think Homer is just a name. Others take him seriously as a genius who assembled the great tales of his time into towering poetry. (The current Favorite Theory: Homer was a Greek-speaking African businessman who collected the stories while sailing around the Mediterranean world.) Whoever he was, or whether or not he was, we have the *Iliad* and the *Odyssey*.

**Like This**: His stories (the *Odyssey* is still one of the best stories ever told, and there are many tales woven in with the catalogues of shields in the *Iliad*), his characters (tricky Odysseus, patient

Penelope, noble Hector, sexy Nausicaa, bad-dude Achilles—even Argos, Odysseus's dog), and his turns of phrase (not just "the wine-dark sea" or "wheel-eyed Athena," but his powers of description). This stuff lives, baby—dead language indeed! Read the *Odyssey* first. If you are among the living, you'll love it.

 Shouldn't there be a 𝔭𝔾ℝ*!!* for him?

Not necessarily, but all right, if you insist. The *Odyssey* starts leisurely, so stick with it. Once the tale-telling starts, you will be very glad you did. I wonder whether there is anything anywhere as moving as the reunion scene between Odysseus and Penelope:

> He was as welcome to her as land to swimmers. . .
> she could not let her white arms drop from his neck.

The *Iliad* is different—a poem of war, detailed, formal, very sad. The Trojan War got Western Civ started, so there is a good reason for learning all about it. 𝔭𝔾ℝ*!!* You can't get close to the original Greek in English, but there are some fine translations. Make no mistake—Homer is worth it.

**Get This**: *The Iliad of Homer.* Translated by Richmond Lattimore. Chicago: Univ. Press, 1975; *Odyssey.* Translated by Robert Fitzgerald. New York: Random House, 1990.

**And How About** *Beowulf*, Dante, the Book of Genesis, *Gilgamesh*, Hesiod, Lucretius, John Milton, Vergil?

### Hughes, Langston (1902 - 1967)

He is often associated with the Harlem Renaissance, a flourishing of arts and culture in the urban African American community between 1920 and 1940. But he was his own man, and he never belonged entirely to anyone else's camp.

**Like This**: Much of his poetry is based on the rhythms and language of jazz and the blues. He gets some lovely effects, using jazz-like improvisations, or refrains and dialect from blues songs.

Had a dream last night I
Thought I was in hell.
I drempt last night I
Thought I was in hell.
Woke up and looked around me—
Babe, your mouth was open like a well.

I said, Baby! Baby!
Please don't snore so loud.
Baby! Please!
Please don't snore so loud.
You jest a little bit o' woman but you
Sound like a great big crowd.

("Morning After")

Hughes also wrote in other idioms, including that of political protest. Favorite themes include oppression and suffering (as in his famous poem "Montage of a Dream Deferred"), history ("The Negro Speaks of Rivers"), identity, and love.

**Get This**: *Selected Poems of Langston Hughes*. New York: Random House, 1990.

**And How About** Amiri Imamu Baraka, Gwendolyn Brooks, Lucille Clifton, Allen Ginsberg, Nikki Giovanni, Carl Sandburg, Ntozake Shange?

## Jonson, Ben (1572 - 1637)

He was a bricklayer, a soldier, a playwright, an actor, and a self-made scholar. Eventually, he left the public stage and wrote "masques," high-class entertainments for the court of King James. He had a way of attracting followers, including poets, courtiers, philosophers, and statesmen. There was even a sort of club, called the Sons of Ben, which spread his ideas and techniques. Until about 1800 his verse and drama were more influential than Shakespeare's.

**Like This**: Most people could open a book of Jonson's poems and just start reading. Most of the poems are short. Most of them are ***occasional***—written for a specific person or event. Perhaps the single most noble and affecting poem on the loss of a child is his.

### On My First Son

Farewell, thou child of my right hand, and joy;
My sin was too much hope of thee, loved boy:
Seven years thou wert lent to me, and I thee pay,
Exacted by thy fate, on the just day.
O could I lose all father now! For why
Will man lament the state he should envy,
To have so soon 'scaped world's and flesh's rage,
And, if no other misery, yet age?
Rest in soft peace, and asked, say, "Here doth lie
Ben Jonson his best piece of poetry."
For whose sake henceforth all his vows be such
As what he loves may never like too much.

𝕻𝕲ℝ!! for some of his poems—but not that many. His poetry is by turns dignified, ironic, funny, and full of praise. The lyric poems and songs from his court masques are amazingly varied and accomplished.

As for the plays—they're hard, harder than Shakespeare's, because most of them are written in the slangy prose of Elizabethan and Jacobean England. But go see them—they live! You will laugh, very hard, at *The Alchemist*, which people do put on (very very occasionally), and his most famous play, *Volpone, or The Fox* (which people put on quite a bit). 𝕻𝕲ℝ!! Ben is someone it pays to get to know.

**Get This**: *Complete Poems*. Edited by George Parfitt. New York: Viking Penguin, 1988. Jonson gets his share of most anthologies of English literature.

**And How About** John Donne, Thom Gunn, George Herbert, Robert Herrick, William Shakespeare?

## Keats, John (1795 - 1821)

He is many people's image of the poet: intense, visionary, and dead before thirty. His dad worked at a stable. (So much for poets being the products of their environments.) The boy did not even try poetry until he was eighteen. Good thing he started then, because he had only eight years left. Suddenly, in 1819, by George, he got it: one of the vintage miracle poetic years. As per the script, he died, famously, of tuberculosis in Rome.

**Like This**: One of my editors puts it this way: "For people in their twenties Keats is the ultimate poet of life and love." He wanted to be original, to avoid influences, and to write about sensations and feelings other poets had missed. His poetry drips with appeals to the senses. In "The Eve of St. Agnes," a dream lover uses such appeals to seduce a virgin. Read the passage below aloud, DR. We'll wait. **DO IT**

> And still she slept an azure-lidded sleep,
> In blanchèd linen, smooth, and lavender'd,
> While he from forth the closet brought a heap
> Of candied apple, quince, and plum, and gourd;
> With jellies soother than the creamy curd,
> And lucent syrups, tinct with cinnamon

Do I have to say anything about the smooth, syrupy, sumptuous music here? He also was a linesmith, crafting many, many lines that are now part of the language: "A thing of beauty is a joy for ever," say, or "Beauty is truth, truth beauty." He really believed that, by the way; he was a high priest for Beauty in all its forms.

With Keats, we are often in a land of myth. Read *Lamia*, which shows he could tell a story. He always remakes his myths, full of burning senses, meanings half-guessed, pain and pleasure and questionings exquisite. I'm starting to write like him.

You can pick up and read most of the shorter poems, but for the longer ones, I'd say PGR*!*

**Get This**: *Keats: Poems*. Selected by J. E. Morpurgo. New York: Viking Penguin, 1985; *Love Poems of John Keats*. New York: St. Martin, 1990. Keats is in most general anthologies.

**And How About** George Gordon, Lord Byron; Hart Crane; Linda Gregg; Wilfred Owen; Wallace Stevens; Alfred, Lord Tennyson; William Wordsworth?

## Koch, Kenneth (1925 - )

Among many other things, this man proves that you can write wonderful poetry at any age. Here he is at seventy, pumping out excellent work. This ambassador for the cause of poetry has taught it to kids in school, the elderly in nursing homes, and to thirty years of poets. He is also a teacher at Columbia University.

**Like This**: I hate and shun labels, but you should know about a group called the "New York Poets." They got started in the 1950s, as part of a movement of sculptors, poets, and painters in a certain East Coast town. God knows what they have in common (these are *very* various poets), but they were looking for a way out of the old and the tired.

Koch found one. His poetry covers the page in long, list-filled, chanting lines of jubilant energy. He is also one of the great comic masters. Really. (Be ready for some strange twists and turns, a great deal of surprise.)

> Is there no voice to cry out from the wind and say what it
> > is like to be the wind,
> To be roughed up by the trees and to bring music from the
> > scattered houses
> And the stones, and to be in such intimate relationship with
> > the sea
> That you cannot understand it? Is there no one who feels
> > like a pair of pants?
> > ("Fresh Air")

**BINGO!** And you can just pick him up and read him. Start anywhere, but two poems I especially love are "Sleeping with Women" and "One Train May Hide Another." He hates stuffiness and anything but the sincere, glad-to-be-telling-you-this approach. And he speaks American.

**Get This**: *One Train: Poems*. New York: Knopf, 1994; *Selected Poems, Nineteen Fifty to Nineteen Eighty-Two*. New York: Random House, 1985.

**And How About** A. R. Ammons, Allen Ginsberg, Gregory Corso, Frank O'Hara, Lawrence Ferlinghetti, Carl Sandburg, Walt Whitman, William Carlos Williams?

## Kooser, Ted (1939 - )

This poet is many people's secret pleasure. He writes moving, unexpected, often funny poems. (See "How to Make Rhubarb Wine," page 51). He's a true product of the Midwest (Iowa and Nebraska, to be mid- about it), and he works for a living, too—as an insurance executive.

**Like This**: The sheer unexpectedness of his ideas.

Rain has beaded the panes
of my office windows,
and in each little lens
the bank at the corner
hangs upside down.
What wonderful music
this rain must have made
in the night, a thousand banks
turned over, the change
crashing out of the drawers
and bouncing upstairs
to the roof, the soft
percussion of ferns
dropping out of their pots
("At the Office Early")

Isn't he great?

**Get This**: *One World at a Time*. Pittsburgh: Univ. Press, 1985;
*Weather Central*. Pittsburgh: Univ. Press, 1994.

**And How About** Julia Kasdorf, Kenneth Koch, Philip Levine,
Peter Meinke, Theodore Roethke?

## **Kumin, Maxine** (1925 - )

She lives on a farm in New Hampshire and writes poetry about
life, farmwork, and God. I want her job.

**Like This**: She writes from a spirit attuned to the natural world.
(Did I mention she is Poet Laureate of New Hampshire?) If you
like animals, nature, and farming, here they are. She watches ani-
mals and their lives very closely, and she learns from them.

Tonight the peepers are a summer camp-
ful of ten-year-olds still shrilling after taps.
Winter will have us back with cold so harsh
the nose hairs freeze. Weasels will spring the traps.
But tonight—tonight the peepers raise the marsh.
("Tonight")

Like all good poets, she's very attentive—in an attractive, open way—to the world around us. I like her optimism, especially about human beings and their place in the world.

> We are not of it, but in it. We are
> in it willynilly with our machinery
> and measurements, and all for the good.
>                                ("Territory")

**You bet.** Get out to the barn, Maxine. I'll stay here and read some of your poems.

**Get This**: *Up Country*: *Poems of New England*. New York: HarperCollins, 1972.

**And How About** Wendell Berry, Robert Frost, Donald Hall, Les Murray, May Sarton, Anne Sexton, Edward Thomas, R. S. Thomas, William Wordsworth?

## Milton, John (1608-1674)

Uh-oh. **PGR!! PGR!! PGR!! PGR!!** I love this man, but you don't have to. He is one of the reasons—and it isn't all his fault—that people feel stupid when it comes to poetry. A man of tremendous talent and learning, he became an ardent Christian-anarchist Puritan; when the Puritans overthrew King Charles, Milton became their Latin Secretary. When the Puritan government fell, Milton's fortunes did too. He spent most of the rest of his life under a kind of house arrest. He lost his eyesight in midlife and (amazing but true) had to dictate *Paradise Lost*, *Paradise Regained*, and later work.

**Like This**: He's not always a ponderous thunderer. "On the Morning of Christ's Nativity" is as lovely a Christmas poem as you could wish. His poems "L'Allegro" and "Il Penseroso" are accomplished looks at happiness and pensiveness. His masque *Comus*, about one heck of a confident virgin, alternates between festive seriousness and serious festivity. Everyone should read at least two of his sonnets: "When I Consider How My Light Is Spent," about losing his sight, and "Methought I Saw My Late Espoused Saint," about a vision of his dead wife.

He wasn't one to aim low, was J. M. His program for *Paradise Lost* was to "justify the ways of God to men." (That's all.) Did he succeed? That's your call. But the attempt created monuments worth the climb: *Paradise Lost*, *Paradise Regained*, and *Samson Agonistes*. Skip *Regained*. Do *Lost*. Satan is truly (and I hate this word) awesome, and Adam and Eve are a **very interesting** couple. **WARNING**: MILTON IS NO GARDEN-VARIETY CHRISTIAN. He has perplexing, provocative takes on God the Father, Christ, and human history.

**PGR!!** *Paradise Lost* can be *Paradise for Footnotes,* too, and is best read with a **Fearless Leader**. Read some of the shorter poems yourself, and take a class for a full tour of *Paradise Lost*.

**Get This**: *The Portable Milton*. Edited by Douglas Bush. New York: Viking Penguin, 1976; *Paradise Lost and Other Poems*. New York: New American Library/Dutton, 1961; *Selected Poems*. New York: Dover, 1993.

**And How About** Dante, The Book of Genesis, Hesiod, Homer, Job, Lucretius, the Psalms, Vergil?

## Moore, Marianne (1887-1972)

One of the great things about reading poetry is meeting some strong, often eccentric personalities. Marianne Moore is a delightful case in point. She went to Bryn Mawr, graduated with a biology degree, and moved to New York with her mom, with whom she lived for the rest of her life. Her reputation as a poet kept on growing until she had won almost every literary prize worth having. She was even invited by the Ford Motor Company to suggest names for their new line of cars. (Then they went ahead and named it the Edsel.) She was a lifelong baseball fan, amateur zoologist, and friend to many people in the arts.

**Like This**: She writes humorous, quirky, pointed poetry about baseball, animals, and machinery. People admire her strange stanza forms and rhyme schemes. Her poetry has wonderful **visual rhythm** as well as sound-games. *Look* at this excerpt from "The Fish" and then **DO** 🏃 **IT** .

## The Fish

wade
through black jade.
  Of the crow-blue mussel-shells, one keeps
  adjusting the ash-heaps;
    opening and shutting itself like

an
injured fan.
  The barnacles which encrust the side
  of the wave, cannot hide
    there for the submerged shafts of the

sun,
split like spun
  glass, move themselves with spotlight swiftness
  into the crevices—
    in and out, illuminating

the
turquoise sea
  of bodies.

There's nobody like her.

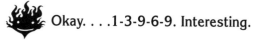 **Whoa! That's some crazy rhyme scheme.** *Swiftness* **and** *crevices*?

She made up her own stanza forms. Count the syllables of each line in each stanza.

**Okay. . . .1-3-9-6-9. Interesting.**

Images abound, always surprising. She had things to say about courage, politics, anteaters, Ireland, and much else. Although she can be brainy, you can pick up her poetry and read it. She's another American original.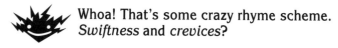

**Get This**: *The Complete Poems*. New York: Viking Penguin, 1987. Marianne Moore is in hundreds of anthologies.

**And How About** e. e. cummings, Ogden Nash, Stevie Smith, William Carlos Williams?

## Murray, Les (1938 - )

Australia is full of good poets, one of whom is Les Murray. He grew up on his father's dairy farm in northern Australia, went to Sydney University, worked as a translator with the Australian National University, and then went back to the farm.

**Like This**: He has written about the environment, nature, farm work, and family life. Anyone interested in Australia, our relation with the earth, or in finding a place in the midst of unstable times, should read him. He is also a master storyteller. He has a very accomplished novel in verse called *The Boys Who Stole the Funeral*. It is written in many different verse forms, yet somehow it still works as a continuous story. (How does he *do* that?) He writes large, wide-open, very clever poetry about life in the only world we've got.

**Get This**: *The Boys Who Stole the Funeral*. New York: Farrar, Straus and Giroux, 1992; *The Rabbiter's Bounty: Collected Poems*. New York: Farrar, Straus and Giroux, 1992.

**And How About** Wendell Berry, Robert Frost, Donald Hall, Maxine Kumin, Edward Thomas, R. S. Thomas, William Wordsworth?

## Nash, Ogden (1902 - 1971)

Everyone knows "Candy is dandy / But liquor is quicker." Ogden Nash, who wrote these lines, later added another: "Pot is not." This delightful poet has a sharp eye and a fund of good things to say. He worked in bond sales, advertising, and teaching before coming to *The New Yorker* magazine and writing his witty verse there and elsewhere for almost four decades.

**Like This**: He *is* funny. How can you read the following excerpt from "Autres Bêtes, Autres Moeurs"—

> The turtle lives 'twixt plated decks
> Which practically conceal its sex.
> I think it clever of the turtle
> In such a fix to be so fertile.

—without a smile? He's mischievously inventive. His lines can be any length at all, but they always end in some extremely telling, often ironic rhyme.

**Get This:** *I Wouldn't Have Missed It: Selected Poems.* New York: Little, 1975; *The Pocket Book of Ogden Nash.* Cutchogue, N.Y.: Buccaneer Books, 1991.

**And How About** W. S. Gilbert, Marianne Moore, Dorothy Parker, Stevie Smith, Judith Viorst?

## Nemerov, Howard (1920 - 1991)

One of the Poets Laureate of the United States, he was born in New York City, got his B.A. at Harvard, and was a pilot for the Canadian and U.S. Air Forces during World War II. He had a distinguished career as a writer and teacher.

**Like This:** He once wrote that the most important things in poetry are "simplicity and the appearance of ease." **You bet!** That's what's so good about him: you can open up a book and begin to read and enjoy. With humor and wit, he writes about history, politics, and his war experience, which he made into an excellent book called *War Stories.* He just kept getting better and better. Unafraid of rhyme or traditional forms, he always uses them well. If you want to know what a well-crafted American contemporary poem can sound like, read Howard Nemerov.

**Get This:** *A Howard Nemerov Reader.* Columbia, Mo.: Univ. of Missouri Press, 1993; *War Stories: Poems about Long Ago and Now.* Chicago: Univ. Press, 1987.

**And How About** Thom Gunn, Seamus Heaney, Anthony Hecht, John Hollander, Robert Pinsky, Karl Shapiro?

## Neruda, Pablo (1904 - 1973)

The twentieth century has seen a huge flowering of poetry in Spanish. Chile's Pablo Neruda is one of the flowers. During a long career as politician and diplomat, he traveled all over the world, especially in Asia and the Americas. He won the Nobel Prize for Literature in 1971. See the film *The Postman (Il Postino)* to see how much he is loved all over the world.

**Like This:** He was a true singer of the material world. I keep his *Twenty Love Poems and a Song of Despair* by the bed. These are haunting love poems, inspired by the verse of the Indian poet Rabindranath Tagore (another one to read!). Neruda also wrote poems about philosophy, history, and politics, some in a difficult modern style.  **PGR!!** *Canto General* is a powerful look at how people live through their lives in the tumult of this century:

> How often, on the winter city streets,
> in a bus, on a ship at twilight, in the most profound
> loneliness—a festival night, surrounded by
> shadows and bells, in the very tomb of human pleasure—
> I have wished to stop, look round for the eternal,
> unfathomable vein I once touched in stone, or in
> the lightning unleashed in a kiss

**BINGO!** His poem *The Heights of Macchu Picchu* ( **PGR!!** )takes us up into the Andes to meditate on this ancient mountain city—and to wonder where civilization came from and where it's going. To the end of his life he wrote love songs and odes to the material things that make life . . . well, life.

**Get This**: *The Heights of Macchu Picchu*: *Bilingual Edition*. Translated by Nathaniel Tarn. New York: Farrar, Straus and Giroux, 1966; *Selected Poems*. New York: Dell, 1973; *Twenty Love Poems and a Song of Despair*. Translated by W. S. Merwin. New York: Viking Penguin, 1993.

**And How About** T. S. Eliot, Nicanor Parra, Octavio Paz, Rabindranath Tagore, César Vallejo?

## Ostriker, Alicia Suskin (1937 - )

Born in New York and educated at Brandeis University and the University of Wisconsin, she is a well-known critic, essayist (especially on William Blake and on women's poetry in America), and poet.

**Like This**: For the most part she writes straight ahead about history, love, and a woman's life—any woman's and her own. Look for "In the Twenty-Fifth Year of Marriage, It Goes On" and "A Meditation in Seven Days." She writes with authority, humor, and a clear eye.

**Get This**: There is a good selection of her poems in *The Pittsburgh Book of Contemporary American Poetry*. Also try *The Imaginary Lover*. Pittsburgh: Univ. Press, 1986; *Once More Out of*

*Darkness*. Berkeley: Berkeley Poets' Workshop and Press, 1974.

**And How About** Ted Kooser, Sharon Olds, Adrienne Rich, Muriel Rukeyser, Anne Sexton, Constance Urdang?

## Ovid [Publius Ovidius Naso] (about 43 B.C. - A.D. 17)

In the time of Augustus Caesar, one of the high points of Roman culture, Ovid was (along with Vergil) the poet of the moment. At the height of his fame, he messed up. We don't know how, but it must have been a very bad career move, because Augustus banished him to the far outposts of the Roman empire. I mean far. I mean what's now Romania.

**Like This:** "Inventive" and "witty" are two words that spring to mind. You read Ovid with a smile of appreciation. Start with the *Metamorphoses*, a good way to introduce yourself to the myths of Greece and Rome, and a good way to become an avid Ovidian.

His erotic poetry—including *The Art of Love*—is some of the best of its kind ever written. No obscenity here. Ovid's interest is in how people come together to make love. *The Art of Love* is a graceful manual of advice. How to apply make-up! How to time insults and rebuffs! When and where to make up a fight!

> When she's been raging at you, when she seems utterly
> > hostile,
> > *Then* is the time to try
> An alliance in bed. She'll come through. Bed's where
> > harmony dwells when
> > The fighting's done: that's the place
> Where loving-kindness was born.
> > (Translated by Peter Green)

Charming.

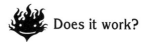 **Does it work?**

Sometimes, DR. With Ovid, the point is less the sex itself than how you get there. He not only is attracted to women but also likes them and how they think.

**Get This:** *The Erotic Poems*. Translated with an introduction and notes by Peter Green. New York: Viking Penguin, 1983;

*Metamorphoses*. Translated by Rolfe Humphries. Bloomington, Ind.: Indiana Univ. Press, 1955.

**And How About** George Gordon, Lord Byron; John Donne; Christopher Marlowe; John Wilmot, Second Earl of Rochester; Theodore Roethke?

## Owen, Wilfred (1893 - 1918)

The First World War made many men and women into brilliant poets. They saw the horror and wrote horribly moving poetry about it. Englishman Wilfred Owen, who was writing warmed-over Keats when war broke out, enlisted and was dropped right into the midst of the Somme. He was sent back home with shell-shock, mended, and returned. A brave soldier, he won the Military Cross before—inevitably, wastefully—the war, only a week from its close, claimed him.

**Like This**: Under the pressure of war, he became an original, uncompromising poet, a wielder of thick, shocking images. He also had a remarkable ear for music, for **slant rhymes**, for dissonant sounds that suggest cataclysm, fear, and rage. His best-known poem depicts a man choking to death on mustard gas. He lets you know that you wouldn't be too sentimental about war

> If in some smothering dreams you too could pace
> Behind the wagon that we flung him in,
> And watch the white eyes writhing in his face,
> His hanging face, like a devil's sick of sin;
> If you could hear, at every jolt, the blood
> Come gargling from the froth-corrupted lungs,
> Obscene as cancer, bitter as the cud
> Of vile, incurable sores on innocent tongues
>> ("Dulce et Decorum Est")

Everyone should read Wilfred Owen and the other poets of World War One. They will challenge you, wrench your stomach—and perhaps make you yearn for peace.

**Get This**: *Poetry of the First World War*. Edited by Edward Hudson. Minneapolis, Minn.: Lerner, 1990.

**And How About** Edmund Blunden, Robert Graves, Randall

Jarrell, David Jones, Yusef Komunyakaa, Isaac Rosenberg, Siegfried Sassoon, Edward Thomas?

## Paz, Octavio (1914 - )

Ambassador, politician, and poet, Paz has become an important part of Mexican history, as well as one of the most prominent world figures in the last half of the twentieth century.

**Like This**: Paz writes in strings of images, sort of an emotional morse code. One image may not have much direct connection with another, but as the images build up, they amount to a tremendously compelling perspective on the world.      **DO IT**

> Like the coral with its branches in the water,
> I send out my senses in this living hour:
> the instant is fulfilled in a yellow harmony—
> oh, noon! wheat-ear heavy with the minutes,
> cup of eternity!
> ("Hymn among the Ruins")

**You bet!** Paz writes about history—human history, Mexican history, third-world history—and about the problem of living a full, valid life in it:      **DO IT**

> We are the monument of a life
> that is someone else's, unlived, hardly ours at all . . .
> —life, when were you ever really ours?
> when are we really what we are?
> In truth, we do not exist, by ourselves
> we are nothing but vertigo, emptiness,
> grimaces in the mirror, horror and vomit,
> life is nothing, we are all
> life—bread of the sun for others,
> all the others we are.
> ("Foot of Stone")

Winner of the Nobel Prize in 1990, he is one of those voices murmuring to the world.

**Get This**: *Collected Poems*. Edited and translated by Eliot Weinberger, with additional translations by Elizabeth Bishop.

New York: New Directions, 1987; *Selected Poems*. Edited by Eliot Weinberger. New York: New Directions, 1984.

**And How About** André Breton, T. S. Eliot, David Gascoyne, Pablo Neruda, César Vallejo?

## Plath, Sylvia (1932 - 1963)

She discovered early that she was a born writer and a woman with a precarious sanity. Her first poems, and her first suicide attempt, occurred before she was a senior at Smith. She attended Cambridge on a Fulbright and met and married the poet Ted Hughes (and you should read him, too). They lived in England and briefly in America while the two made a living through teaching and writing. In 1962 she had a second child, her marriage collapsed, and she began to write as she never had before, with fiery genius and speed, turning out more than forty poems (most of them were published in a book titled *Ariel*). In the winter of 1963, her depression reached a nadir and took her life.

**Like This:** I wish people could forget the tabloid-headline quality of her death and just sit down with her poetry. "Daddy" and "Lady Lazarus" are shocking, desperate, violent, original poems. Of course they are statements of terrible personal pain—and that is one reason to read them. But they also explore life and its spiritual hardships with disturbing clarity.

She does write about hope. In poems such as "The Bee Meeting," she admires the hard-working bees who find ways to survive (as she did not) the winter. And Plath is also a poet of the unnoticed beauties in life, as in this excerpt from "Black Rook in Rainy Weather." Moments of joy are small and hard-won, but they're there.

**DO IT**

> With luck,
> Trekking stubborn through this season
> Of fatigue, I shall
> Patch together a content
>
> Of sorts. Miracles occur,
> If you care to call those spasmodic
> Tricks of radiance miracles.

But I guess people will always remember her bitter nursery rhymes that explore desperation. Her speakers like to be the center of attention, showing off in the midst of great pain.

> I think I am going up,
> I think I may rise———
> The beads of hot metal fly, and I, love, I
>
> Am a pure acetylene
> Virgin
> Attended by roses,
>
> By kisses, by cherubim,
> By whatever these pink things mean.
> Not you, nor him
>
> Not him, nor him
> (My selves dissolving, old whore petticoats)———-
> To Paradise.
>
> ("Fever 103°")

Her poetry can teach us what it means to suffer, to be made of regret. These poems are not "about her life"—they speak of all lives that are denied.

**Get This**: *Ariel*. New York: HarperCollins, 1981; *Collected Poems*. Edited by Ted Hughes. New York: HarperCollins, 1981.

**And How About** W. H. Auden, Emily Dickinson, H.D., Ted Hughes, Robert Lowell, Alicia Ostriker, Adrienne Rich, Theodore Roethke, Anne Sexton, Stevie Smith, W. D. Snodgrass, W. B. Yeats?

## Poe, Edgar Allan (1809 - 1849)

Poe is famous for his tortured life, made more tortured by addiction to alcohol. Orphaned at three, he was raised for a time in England. He was a newspaper writer for a while, and then tried to earn a living as a freelance journalist (which was easier to do then—but never very easy for him). After his wife's death, his never-too-firmly-hinged mind slipped off the peg, little by little.

**Like This**: The rhythms and music of his poems. Even when they don't mean much (which is often), they communicate lurid horror, raging madness, murderous vengefulness, hopeless longing. Many are just barely in Poe's control. People remember his poetry; it stays with them with a kind of dark morbid power. Poe is nothing if not vivid. Can you forget that big black bird? Or the bells ringing in your head? Poe helped create the murder mystery and the tale of horror and suspense. Stoke the fire, turn down the lights, and perform a few of his poems, and you and your friends can walk the dark, winding streets, haggard, staring, hopeless, endlessly, madly repeating . . . uh, what was it the bird quoth?

**Get This**: *The Raven and Other Poems*. New York: Scholastic, 1992.

**And How About** Samuel Taylor Coleridge; Robert Frost; George MacBeth; Christina Rossetti; Alfred, Lord Tennyson?

## Psalms (900 - 500 B.C.)

Sacred scriptures of all religions contain some of the most beautiful poetry ever made. Atop this treasure-trove is the Book of Psalms, an anthology of hymns composed or translated by Hebrew poets over the centuries.

**Like This**: These are uplifting, muscular poems about humanity's relationships with God.

> The Lord is my shepherd; I shall not want;
> he makes me lie down in green pastures.
> He leads me beside still waters;
> he restores my soul.
> 
> (Psalm 23)

And it's not always a picnic having a God in your world:

> Why do you stand so far off, O Lord,
> and hide your face in the needful time of trouble?
> 
> (Psalm 10)

Mostly the Psalms are intoxicated with the power of the Author of the universe:

The heavens declare the glory of God,
    and the firmament shows his handiwork.
                    (Psalm 19)

**BINGO!** These ancient Hebrew poems are also part of our English-speaking heritage. As translated in the King James Bible or the Book of Common Prayer, they are some of our earliest and best examples of **free verse**! Even a stone atheist can pick up the Good Book and get drunk on the sheer poetry of the Psalms. **DO IT**

**Get This**: Your friendly neighborhood Bible. Or *The Psalms*. Translated by Nicholas De Lange and edited by Peter Levi. New York: Viking Penguin, 1986.

**And How About** Ecclesiastes, Isaiah, Jeremiah, Job, Proverbs, the Song of Solomon? And the Koran, full of sublime poetry?

## Pushkin, Aleksandr (1799 -1837)

During his short life, he wrote everything from lyric poems to national epics. He had a rocky marriage, but when his wife was insulted, he fought a duel to defend her honor. Bad career move. Or good one: he became an instant legend, the voice of the Russian soul.

**Like This**: He appears to have simply *thought* in poetry. Even in translation you can sense his mastery of language, his playfulness, and his range. A born storyteller, he can set a scene, a mood, a theme, and create characters to match. Start with *Eugene Onegin*, a tale of love, dreams, and tragedy, told with a curious mixture of detachment and humane sympathy. Such characters!: Eugene, the man who is tired of being everywhere and doing everything; Tatyana, the girl who watches the moon, hopelessly in love with Eugene. Pushkin wrote for people to read him. You can pick up any of the shorter poems or *Eugene Onegin* and **DO IT**.

**Get This**: *Collected Narrative and Lyrical Poetry*. Translated by Walter Arndt. Ann Arbor, Mich.: Ardis, 1984; *Eugene Onegin: A Novel in Verse*. Translated by Vladimir Nabokov. Princeton: Univ. Press, 1990.

**And How About** Anna Akhmatova; George Gordon, Lord Byron;

Robert Frost; Johann Wolfgang von Goethe; John Keats; Robert Pinsky; Vikram Seth; William Wordsworth?

## **Rich, Adrienne** (1929 - )

Born in Baltimore, she graduated from Radcliffe, married, and had three children. But her life changed when American politics began to heave up in the 1960s. She protested first against the Vietnam War, and then against the treatment of women in modern society. Through her poetry, books, teaching, and lecturing, she has become one of the leading voices in the American feminist movement, as well as one of the most widely read and imitated poets in America.

**Like This**: Her early poems were tight, formal, witty; in the 1960s she started to experiment with new ways of throwing a poem together. Wit gives way to anger and protest, and tight structure and rhyme give way to collages of images.

> I have been standing all my life in the
> direct path of a battery of signals
> the most accurately transmitted most
> untranslatable language in the universe
> I am a galactic cloud so deep     so invo-
> luted that a light wave could take 15
> years to travel through me     And has
> taken     I am an instrument in the shape
> of a woman trying to translate pulsations
> into images     for the relief of the body
> and the reconstruction of the mind.
>                 ("Planetarium")

 **Whew! That could be about poetry, politics—or just about being a woman.**

**You bet**, DR. She writes of how speaking creates history, and how people need to speak. Anger is there, but it's a channeled anger. Her most recent work (*An Atlas of the Difficult World*) has a beautiful mastery. Because she can get pretty brainy, ℙ𝔾ℝ*!!* to get the most out of her poetry, even though she has plenty of poems (see "Song," page 60) that are immediately readable. She found a new way to write, that's all.

**Get This**: *An Atlas of the Difficult World: Poems, 1988-1991.* New York: Norton, 1991; *Diving into the Wreck: Poems, 1971-1972.* New York: Norton, 1994; *The Dream of a Common Language: Poems, 1974-1977.* New York: Norton, 1993.

**And How About** W. H. Auden, Elizabeth Bishop, Robert Lowell, Sylvia Plath, Anne Sexton, W. B. Yeats?

## Roethke, Theodore (1908 - 1963)

This natural singer was born in Michigan and taught at Penn State; the extremely famous Lafayette College in Easton, Pa.; Bennington; and the University of Washington. He battled depression and alcoholism all his life.

**Like This**: You can pick him up and read him.

> The whiskey on your breath
> Could make a small boy dizzy;
> But I hung on like death:
> Such waltzing was not easy.
> ("My Papa's Waltz")

That's Roethke: musical, musical, full of humor, but never turning away from the hardships of life (in "My Papa's Waltz," father and son dance, revealing the trappings of a tough life: "You beat time on my head / With a palm caked hard by dirt").

He sees joy and pain, pleasure and death, with eyes wide open. And he is one of the very best love poets of the century, says Harold Fenniman of Dog's Leg, Utah.

> We sing together; we sing mouth to mouth.
> The garden is a river flowing south.
> She cries out loud the soul's own secret joy;
> She dances, and the ground bears her away.
> She knows the speech of light, and makes it plain
> A lively thing can come to life again.
> ("She")

**BINGO! Uh-huh! You bet!** Such energy in life, Ted! Such joyful sexiness! I'm not quoting any of his painful poetry, but it's just as knowing, just as good. Roethke sees the Spirit in everything. He suffers a personal journey through darkness into new light. No one I'd rather recommend, DR.

**Get This:** *Collected Poems.* New York: Doubleday, 1975. Roethke is in all good anthologies of American poetry. If he's not in 'em, they ain't good.

**And How About** W. H. Auden, Louise Bogan, Catullus, Stanley Kunitz, Ovid, Sylvia Plath, Sappho, William Wordsworth, W. B. Yeats?

## Rogers, Pattiann (1940 - )

Her poetry often begins with observation of the natural world—and ends up considering the human world. Our connectedness with nature is her theme, but then, so is love.

**Like This:** Rogers draws on a wide-ranging knowledge of science for her poems. They make surprising connections, waking you up to the hidden miraculousness of the outside world—and the hidden miracles inside, too.

**Get This:** *Firekeeper: New and Selected Poems.* Minneapolis, Minn.: Milkweed Editions, 1994.

**And How About** Marianne Moore, Mary Oliver, May Sarton, Elizabeth Anne Socolow, William Carlos Williams?

## Rukeyser, Muriel (1913 - 1980)

One of America's fine midcentury poets, she lived in New York and was very active in political causes between 1930 and 1980.

**Like This:** Read her poem "Effort at Speech between Two People." She writes about flying (she was a pilot), feminism (she is one of the formative influences on feminist literature in the United States), and politics. But she also writes about love and modern life. She is a well-kept secret, except among those who know good poetry.

**Get This:** *Out of Silence: Selected Poems.* Edited by Kate Daniels. Evanston, Ill.: TriQuarterly, 1992.

**And How About** W. H. Auden, Horace Gregory, Rolfe Humphries, Audre Lorde, Hugh MacDiarmid, Adrienne Rich, Anne Sexton?

**Sappho** (around 600 B.C.)
We have only fragments of her poems—but they are so sweet, you wonder what the whole thing was like. Sappho was one of the earliest Greek lyric poets. She lived on the island of Lesbos, where, for the most part, she wrote songs of love. In fact, she wrote a famous poem arguing that love was a more fitting subject for poetry than war.

**Like This**: She is passionate, fresh, and surprising. In the throes of longing for a loved one, she writes

> a trembling seizes my body
> I am paler than grass
> in my mania, little better than dead

She prays to Aphrodite to bring her lover around, and she imagines Aphrodite replying

> Well!
> If she ignores you now, soon she'll chase you;
> If she rejects your gifts, soon she'll be giving them;
> If she's not in love now, soon she will be,
>                           Against her will.

As I said, she's mostly in fragments, but such fragments!

**Get This**: *Sappho: A New Translation* by Mary Barnard. Berkeley: Univ. of California Press, 1958.

**And How About** Elizabeth Barrett Browning, Catullus, John Donne, Robert Graves, H.D., Adrienne Rich, Sir Philip Sidney?

**Seth, Vikram** (1952- )
Quick: what's the best-selling novel in English in the past hundred years written entirely in poetry?

 *The Golden Gate* by **Vikram Seth.**

You peeked. Born in India, educated in England, China, and the United States, he writes accomplished, quiet, graceful poetry on a variety of topics. He also has written children's poetry and *A*

*Suitable Boy*, a giga-bestseller twenty-pound novel set in India.

**Like This**: *The Golden Gate* tells the tale of young adults living in San Francisco in the mid-1980s. Seth has it down: the city, the countryside, the worries and pleasures and loves and loneliness. And somehow he makes it all work in *poetry*. (How does he *do* that?)

His other poetry is similarly delightful. *All You Who Sleep Tonight* contains poems on love, friendship (one of his great themes), suffering, and comfort. He aims to write poetry that engages your head and heart without being academic or difficult—a poetry full of feeling but handled unponderously. He's doing it, and we should all be glad. ▟▟▟▟▟▟ **DO** 🏃 **IT**

**Get This**: *All You Who Sleep Tonight*. New York: Random House, 1991; *The Golden Gate*. New York: Random House, 1987.

**And How About** Dana Gioia, George Herbert, Howard Nemerov, Timothy Steele, Rabindranath Tagore, Yvor Winters?

## Shakespeare, William (1564 - 1616)

Every day, most English-speaking people speak at least one or two phrases of his. There must be a reason for that—maybe that he was just plain good. Son of a glove-maker, he came to London around his eighteenth year and worked his way into acting, producing, and writing. When the plague closed the theaters, he found a patron (we think) who paid him to write poetry (get *me* that job!). Somewhere in there he wrote the sonnets, about as good as sonnets get. Then you have a play or two that was semi-decent. He died a pretty well-off middle-class fellow.

**Like This**: Bill was Bill. Get used to it. He wrote at great speed, didn't revise much, just dipped his quill, said to himself, "Hmmmmm . . . *Ham* . . . *let*," and started writing away. Makes you want to give up writing. His great talent, says Gus Torag of Chortling Ridge, Connecticut, lay in making points of view *real*. Whether it is the loving, idealistic, cynical, tortured, ecstatic speaker of his sonnets or the raging of Othello, he could create imaginary people and make them live in our brains. No half-measures here—he tries for, and often achieves, the utmost in emotional impact. Images everywhere, and one of the all-time ears for rhythm and music. Combine all that, and you have the world's most famous poet.

Really, DR, there is nothing to fear and everything to enjoy in him. Go see some plays—or see the movies and then the plays. Buy the *Sonnets* and leave them around the house. They'll get read.

**Get This**: *The Sonnets*. New York: New American Library/Dutton, 1964. Any of the Folger or Signet editions of his plays are good. If you want a collected, you might get *Complete Works of William Shakespeare*. Edited by David M. Bevington. New York: HarperCollins, 1992; or *The Riverside Shakespeare*. Edited by G. Blakemore Evans. Boston: Houghton Mifflin, 1974. But the idea is to **DO IT**. Otherwise, get out of my book.

**And How About** William Blake, Emily Dickinson, John Donne, T. S. Eliot, Ben Jonson, John Keats, Christopher Marlowe, Sir Philip Sidney, William Wordsworth, Sir Thomas Wyatt, W. B. Yeats?

## Smith, Stevie (1902 -1971)

There is a good movie called *Stevie*, starring Glenda Jackson as the poet Stevie Smith. From the age of three until her death, she lived in the same house with her maiden aunt. She worked at a publishing house until her fifties, after which she lived on her writing.

**Like This**: She often uses nursery-rhyme forms to explore very serious things. She shifts abruptly from childish to adult voices, from humor to seriousness. Her poems cover a wide range of topics, but many of them look at religion and death. As for the first, she goes back and forth, from yes to no, almost in the same line. The second topic, death, became a growing preoccupation.

Nobody heard him, the dead man,
But still he lay moaning:
I was much further out than you thought
And not waving but drowning.
                    ("Not Waving but Drowning")

With Stevie Smith, you often don't know whether to laugh or cry. She wanted it that way. There is no one else like her.

**Get This**: *Collected Poems*. Edited by James MacGibbon. New York: New Directions, 1983.

**And How About** Richard Armour, W. H. Auden, Emily Dickinson, Marianne Moore, Ogden Nash, Sylvia Plath?

**Tennyson, Alfred [Alfred, Lord Tennyson]** (1809-1892)
Tennyson tried to write poetry that spoke about, for, and to people everywhere. He did it for most of the Victorian era and made a very nice living from it. He was made Poet Laureate in 1850.

**Like This**: There is much to like in Tennyson because there is much of Tennyson. He wrote poems about evolution, feminism, colonialism, technology, urban blight, and social inequality. He also wrote tremendous love poems, *soliloquies* (speeches by one person—like "Ulysses" and "Maud"), Arthurian romances (*The Idylls of the King*), and *occasional* verse. What was he good at? Anything. He can really set a scene. He is one of the best of all descriptive poets. (Read "The Eagle: A Fragment," page 40.) He can appeal to all of the senses in some pretty sexy music.

**DO IT**

> Now slides the silent meteor on, and leaves
> A shining furrow, as thy thoughts in me.
>
> Now folds the lily all her sweetness up,
> And slips into the bosom of the lake.
> So fold thyself, my dearest, thou, and slip
> Into my bosom and be lost in me.
> ("Now Sleeps the Crimson Petal")

**Uh-huh!** I mean, why only "The Charge of the Light Brigade"? The worst thing that ever happened to Tennyson was the death of Arthur Hallam, his mentor and close friend at Cambridge. For seventeen years he worked on a great poem about Hallam's death, and *In Memoriam* is it. This poem takes on death, grief, evolution, geology, the cosmos, and the existence of God. Other than that, it doesn't do too much. What's best is you can read the thing. A course in Victorian poetry would help, but for the most part, Tennyson's voice is still as deep-chested and clear today as it was when he wrote.

**Get This**: *In Memoriam*. Edited by Robert H. Ross. New York: Norton, 1974; *In Memoriam, Maud, and Other Poems*. Boston: Tuttle, 1991; *Selected Poems*. New York: Dover, 1992.

**And How About** Elizabeth Barrett Browning, Robert Browning, T. S. Eliot, Edward FitzGerald, Robert Frost, Gerard Manley Hopkins, Christina Rossetti, R. S. Thomas?

## Thomas, R. S. (1913 - )

For most of his life he was a country minister in Wales. Many of his poems are written about that hard, stony country and its people. He sympathizes with the poor; he hates their empty-headedness, but doesn't blame it on them.

**Like This**: All of the above. This man writes very musical poetry, even when the poetry is rough and bleak. That's because Thomas studied Welsh and has absorbed the beautiful music of that language. His is some of the best poetry about doubt and belief that you can find. He applies science and human experience to the question of God; you can sense a man giving all of himself without being either sentimental or moralistic about it.

**Get This**: *Poems of R. S. Thomas*. Fayetteville, Ark.: Univ. of Arkansas Press, 1985.

**And How About** Wendell Berry, Robert Frost, Ted Hughes, Maxine Kumin, Philip Larkin, Dylan Thomas, Edward Thomas?

## Updike, John (1932 - )

People think of him as a fine novelist and a very fine essayist, but the man is a pretty good poet, too.

**Like This**: His poetry is accessible and full of experience. Lately, he has been writing honest, heartbreaking poems about aging. (Read "Elderly Sex," page 63.)

**Get This**: *Collected Poems, 1953-1993*. New York: Knopf, 1993; *Midpoint and Other Poems*. New York: Knopf, 1969; *Telephone Poles and Other Poems*. New York: Knopf, 1963.

**And How About** Louise Bogan, Donald Hall, Donald Justice?

## Vergil [Publius Vergilius Maro] (70 - 19 B.C.)

The Greeks had Homer and the Romans had Vergil. He seems to have taken his poetic career very slowly and very traditionally, starting with poetry about shepherds (the *Eclogues*) and poetry about farmers (the *Georgics*) before tackling his great work, the *Aeneid*. Vergil, lucky man, was supported by Maecenas, a moneybags who liked to endow poets' work. Augustus himself encouraged Vergil to work on the *Aeneid*. Vergil was supposed to be an extreme perfectionist who counted it a good day if he had completed a single line. When he had his great poem nearly complete, he went on a trip. Bad career move.

**Like This**: The *Eclogues* speak of the country life and how it never seems to last. They are a good introduction to Vergil. The *Aeneid* tells of Aeneas, a Trojan who escapes his burning city and goes on adventures around the world until he comes to rest in Italy and founds the colony that will become Rome. He battles monsters, gods, and love (he woos and then jilts Dido, Queen of Carthage) and descends into the underworld. All that to get history started! A great story. What *I* like best is Aeneas himself—an odd sort of hero, a trifle reluctant to take on all this responsibility. But again and again he sees that fate, history, and the gods are saying **DO IT**, and he does. My favorite scene: Aeneas carrying his father Anchises out of flaming Troy.

At one time—for centuries!—Vergil was the basis of a thinking person's education. After Homer, open Vergil.

**Get This**: *Aeneid*. Translated by Robert Fitzgerald. New York: Random House, 1990; *The Eclogues*. Translated by Guy Lee. New York: Viking Penguin, 1984; *Georgics*. Translated by Smith P. Bovie. Chicago: Univ. Press, 1966.

**And How About** *Beowulf*, Dante, Ed Dorn, the Book of Genesis, *Gilgamesh*, Hesiod, Homer, Lucretius, John Milton?

## Verlaine, Paul (1844 - 1896)

He started out as a civil servant, but he kept scribbling and by twenty-five was a well-known poet. In famously decadent manner, he cohabited and uncohabited with Arthur Rimbaud, after which he returned to Catholicism and made a living as a critic, essayist, and poet.

**Like This**: French poetry lives in its vowel sounds, and Verlaine had them in his nervous system. In ravishingly delicate music, he creates a world of symbols that direct us to feelings. **DO IT**

> Your soul is an exquisite landscape
> Where charming masques and bergamasques
> Play the lute and dance, somehow
> Sad under their fantastic disguises.

Singing in minor keys
Of love the conqueror and life full of treasures,
They seem not to believe in their happiness,
And their song melts in the moonlight,

The still moonlight, sad and lovely,
Which makes the birds dream in the trees
And the fountains sob with ecstasy,
The great fountains, slim among the statues.

("Moonlight")

He conjures up sadness and longing in this scene. Believe me, you lose an orchestra of sensitive sounds in the translation—but you do get the wonderful images, a sense of how Verlaine works.

**Get This**: *Selected Poems*. Translated by C. F. MacIntyre. Berkeley: Univ. of California Press, 1948.

**And How About** Charles Baudelaire, Paul Claudel, Hart Crane, Stéphane Mallarmé, Arthur Rimbaud, Wallace Stevens, Paul Valéry?


## Whitman, Walt (1819-1892)

Born in Long Island, he was a journalist, teacher, Civil War nurse, vagabond, and government clerk. But those were just his day jobs.

**Like This**: With his sweeping, all-inclusive, life-affirming poetry, this man is America on paper. Few poets since have been totally free of his influence. He sees everything in himself, himself in everything, and invites you along. And guess what? You can read him. Open any page and start. **DO IT**

It avails not, time nor place—distance avails not,
I am with you, you men and women of a generation, or ever so
    many generations hence,
Just as you feel when you look on the river and sky, so I
    felt,
Just as any of you is one of a living crowd, I was one of a
    crowd,
Just as you are refresh'd by the gladness of the river and
    the bright flow, I was refresh'd,

Just as you stand and lean on the rail, yet hurry with the
    swift current, I stood yet was hurried,
Just as you look on the numberless masts of ships and the
    thick-stemm'd pipes of steamboats, I look'd.
                              ("Crossing Brooklyn Ferry")

**BINGO!** **You bet!** He speaks American, DR. He's oceanic, coast-to-coast big—but his heart is the same size as yours. What he shall assume you shall assume.

**Get This**: It's not exactly hard to find old Walt. He's in most anthologies of American poetry. (He's usually the first *third* of most anthologies of American poetry.) Also there is *Leaves of Grass*. Edited by Bradley E. Sculley and Harold W. Blodgett. New York: Norton, 1973; *Selected Poems*. New York: Dover, 1991.

**And How About** A. R. Ammons, Allen Ginsberg, Albert Goldbarth, Langston Hughes, Pablo Neruda, Robert Pinsky, Pattiann Rogers, Carl Sandburg, William Carlos Williams?

## Williams, William Carlos (1883 - 1963)

He wrote a few lines that could be the motto for this book:

                          It is difficult
          to get the news from poems
                    yet men die miserably every day
                        for lack
        of what is found there.
                        (*Asphodel, That Greeny Flower*)

 **Double Bingo!!**

**You bet**, DR. He was both a general practitioner in Rutherford, New Jersey, and a thoroughly American poet.

**Like This**: He is open to everything. He speaks straightforward American. His poems are bracing, stripped, and direct. He can dance naked in front of a mirror, as in "Danse Russe." He can see America for the confused mess it sometimes is, as in "To Elsie." He is a superb poet of description, as in any of his famous poems about trees and flowers. What makes *them* so good is their precision, as in "The Rose": "The rose is obsolete / but each petal ends in / an edge, the double facet / cementing the grooved / columns of air."

**BINGO!** You bet! Urban life is another of his subjects, as in his epic poem *Paterson*—that's right, an epic, and an excellent one, about Paterson, New Jersey. And if his poem *Asphodel, That Greeny Flower* isn't the best love poem of the century (again, original—he wrote it to his wife), it's up there. Read him aloud and smile.

**Get This**: *Asphodel, That Greeny Flower, and Other Love Poems.* New York: New Directions, 1994; *Selected Poems.* Edited and with an introduction by Charles Tomlinson. New York: New Directions, 1985.

**And How About** Robert Frost, Allen Ginsberg, Albert Goldbarth, Robert Lowell, Mark Strand, Charles Tomlinson, Walt Whitman?


## Wordsworth, William (1770 - 1850)

Because of him, many people *still* think of a poet as a person who languishes in a meadow, moaning, "Ah, nature!" *Donnez-moi un break!* Born in the Lake District in England, he grew up surrounded by nature. He attended Cambridge and went on walking tours of France and Wales. In 1798 he wrote a book (with Samuel Taylor Coleridge) called *Lyrical Ballads*, which started something new. In 1843 he was made Poet Laureate. He lived with his sister Dorothy (his devoted champion, secretary, and traveling companion) for almost sixty years.

**Like This**: His stories of doubt, love, and communion with nature. Four of them, called "the Lucy poems," are especially striking. Here's one.

### A Slumber Did My Spirit Seal

A slumber did my spirit seal;
   I had no human fears:
She seemed a thing that could not feel
   The touch of earthly years.

No motion has she now, no force;
   She neither hears nor sees;
Rolled round in earth's diurnal course,
   With rocks, and stones, and trees.

Love and pain folded into the rolling forth of the universe. Read his tales about shepherds, cottagers, and ramblers in the Lake District. Not all scenery, they are often disturbing tales of loss and love and worry. And then there are the many poems drunk with the holy spirit of nature. We can achieve our best selves if we pay attention to that spirit.

Therefore am I still
A lover of the meadows and the woods,
And mountains; and of all that we behold
From this green earth
         ("Lines Composed a Few
          Miles above Tintern Abbey")

After lunch some time, read aloud "Ode: Intimations of Immortality from Recollections of Early Childhood." Bearing you off on the power of its vision, it explores how near a child's soul is to the bliss of Paradise.

Wordsworth also produced a gigantic poem called *The Prelude*, a spiritual autobiography in verse. PGR!!

**Get This**: *Favorite Poems*. New York: Dover, 1992; *The Prelude: Seventeen Ninety-Nine, Eighteen Hundred and Five, Eighteen Fifty*. Edited by Jonathan Wordsworth. New York: Norton, 1979; *Selected Poems*. New York: Random House, 1993.

**And How About** A. R. Ammons; Wendell Berry; George Gordon, Lord Byron; Samuel Taylor Coleridge; John Keats; Pattiann Rogers; Percy Bysshe Shelley; Jon Silkin, Charles Tomlinson?

## Yeats, William Butler (1865 - 1939)

People ask me all the time, "John, who is this century's greatest poet?" No answer here, baby. Most of the poetry lovers I know, however, would name Yeats. Romantic, modern, revolutionary, mystic, Yeats became (and still is) one of the most influential poets in history. He won the Nobel Prize in 1923.

**Like This**: Yeats is not so very hard to read. He has a few weird aspects, but most of the time you can follow him. He is yet another poet whose words become absolutely enchanting read aloud. Yes, he was into the occult and developed a mystical, semi-loony theory of history (events repeat themselves in cycles or "gyres"). For that reason, 𝔓𝔾ℜ*!!* for his modern poems—but I tell you, most of these you could read by yourself. He is also a great love poet—

**DO** ⚡ **IT**

> When you are old and gray and full of sleep,
> And nodding by the fire, take down this book,
> And slowly read, and dream of the soft look
> Your eyes had once, and of their shadows deep
>                                   ("When You Are Old")

—and a great poet on growing old. He wrote penetrating poems about the Irish struggle ("September 1913," "Easter 1916") and about Irish myth and folklore.

"The Circus Animals' Desertion" sums up his career. It's a good example of his later poetry: profound, rock-hard, colloquial, modern, wild. He sees his own life as

**DO** ⚡ **IT**

> A mound of refuse or the sweepings of a street,
> Old kettles, old bottles, and a broken can,
> Old iron, old bones, old rags, that raving slut
> Who keeps the till. Now that my ladder's gone,
> I must lie down where all the ladders start,
> In the foul rag-and-bone shop of the heart.

What a magician of sound. His lines—Yeats wrote the verse above when he was around seventy-three!—glow, that's all, they glow. Do it, do it, do it.

**Get This**: *Selected Poems*. New York: Random House, 1992.

**And How About** W. H. Auden, William Blake, Louise Bogan, Austin Clarke, Dante, T. S. Eliot, H.D., Seamus Heaney, James Joyce, Philip Larkin, Louis MacNeice, Marianne Moore, Ezra Pound?

### It breaks my heart to stop. So many poets deserve to be here.

# A WHOLE PAGE FULL OF POETS WRITING TODAY YOU MIGHT LIKE TO READ

**So WHAT** if you don't know some of these poets?
Wait until you read a few of their poems.

Diane Ackerman
Ben Belitt
Frank Bidart
Lucille Clifton
Alfred Corn
Stephen Dobyns
Rita Dove
Norman Dubie
Russell Edson
Carolyn Forché
Dana Gioia
Louise Glück
Debora Greger
Linda Gregerson
Linda Gregg
Thom Gunn
Jim Harrison
Robert Hass
Edward Hirsch
Linda Hogan
Garrett Hongo
Donald Justice
Galway Kinnell
Yusef Komunyakaa
Greg Kuzma
Brad Leithauser
Philip Levine
William Matthews
James McMichael

Sandra McPherson
Sharon Olds
Mary Oliver
Jay Parini
Linda Pastan
Molly Peacock
Robert Pinsky
Katha Pollitt
Bin Ramke
Alberto Ríos
Sherod Santos
Beth Seetch
Alan Shapiro
Charles Simic
Louis Simpson
Dave Smith
Gary Snyder
Elizabeth Ann Socolow
Timothy Steele
Mark Strand
Charles Tomlinson
Chase Twichell
Lee Upton
Mona Van Duyn
David Wagoner
Anne Waldman
Richard Wilbur
C. K. Williams
Charles Wright

# PLACES YOU MIGHT FIND THEIR POETRY

*The American Poetry Review*
*The Antioch Review*
*Beloit Poetry Journal*
*The Black Warrior Review*
*Boston Review*
*Chicago Review*
*Colorado Review*
*Crazyhorse*
*Field*
*The Gettysburg Review*
*Grand Street*
*The Hudson Review*
*The Iowa Review*
*The Kenyon Review*
*New American Writing*
*New England Review*
*Northwest Review*
*The Ohio Review*
*On the Bus*
*Painted Bride Quarterly*

*Ploughshares*
*Poetry: A Magazine of Verse*
*Poetry East*
*Poetry Flash*
*Poetry New York*
*River Styx*
*Salmagundi*
*Sequoia*
*Shenandoah*
*Southern Poetry Review*
*The Southern Review*
*Southwest Review*
*The Threepenny Review*
*TriQuarterly*
*The Virginia Quarterly Review*
*Western Humanities Review*
*Writers' Open Forum*
*The Yale Review*
*ZYZZYVA*

And there are hundreds more—especially what are known as the "little magazines" or "small press magazines." These have some of the best new poets. You have to look for them in bookstores devoted to literature and local culture.

## Epilogue:
# A Word from Your Trusty Guide

**P**oetry changes people's lives.

Take it from a guy who knows.

On an autumn Saturday in Orange, California, in the troubled year of 1968, nothing was doing at home, so I jumped on my Stingray and rode down the street. At fifteen, despite my friends and my massively Irish family, I was solitary and out of register. *Sergeant Pepper's Lonely Hearts Club Band* played on every other car radio. Social ferment charged the air, as did the paralysis and outrage of Vietnam, yet Orange, in the American suburban tradition, snoozed on.

Pedaling, I wondered, "What's going to happen to me? What will I become? What kind of world will I live in?" Mine was the song of Naquali: "I wonder what my future life **/** will do to me."

Turning down the wide, sleepy street where all the churches are, I parked at the new branch library, an odd, two-story octagonal building with broad windows. I noticed a sliver of moon in the afternoon sky and went in.

Nobody around, except for a single librarian who grimaced through me as I entered. After five minutes, she slipped into her office. All to myself, a library illuminated by an uncanny autumn light.

Where to begin? I was drawn—I don't remember how—to the poetry shelf, which sagged with no less than seven volumes. I took the first one, the biggest, an anthology of American poetry, and sat down.

Was it the October light? the words? the questions jangling inside me on that day of decision all over the world except for me? I remember beginning to read and being taken in, forgetting I was there, time passing, the angle of light growing more and more acute as I read. Edgar Lee Masters, Edward Arlington Robinson, Muriel Rukeyser ("Effort at Speech Between Two People" spoke to me: "Speak to me. Take my hand. What are you now? / I will tell you all. I will conceal nothing."); e. e. cummings, Don Marquis, Amy Lowell, Robert Lowell, Elizabeth Bishop, Robert Frost, Archibald MacLeish, Walt Whitman, Emily Dickinson, Wallace Stevens. New lives connected with mine in the North American idiom.

Never before had so many emotions arrived with such force, such clarity, such precision. I discovered complexities of feeling I didn't know existed. I didn't know you could write poems about slaughterhouses, or paying bills, or arguments, or Einstein (there's a wonderful MacLeish poem about him), or sex (I was shocked), or trout.

I was watching the expansion of my world; in this moment, my understanding was growing to take in a newly enriched universe. Rocking back and forth in time and subject and tone, I was clearing out a wider space in which to construct my coming self. I laughed at the librarian (if she only knew what was going on). After a few hours, I was so charged that I looked up from the page and seemed to levitate in the library.

I read all seven poetry books that little library had. I was glad people fell in love; others were making a big mistake, and I wanted to warn them; I pitied those who deluded themselves that God existed; I realized what the universe must look like to God; I resolved to be good; I resolved to be cruel in my own self-interest; I was terrified of hell; I wished my father would dance with me once; I decided to be a rodeo clown; I decided to be an iron-smelter; I decided to be a surgeon; I decided to be president; I saw that all men were brothers; I saw that all men were hopelessly alone; I wanted to eat a peach.

"Five o'clock. Closing time." The librarian, playing her role. Out I went, disoriented, full of omnidirectional resolutions, to vibrate my way back home in the almost-dark.

Before riding to the library, I had been a boy afraid of the disorder in the universe. I was still that boy, but as I rode back, I knew I had allowed a new stage to begin. Someday I would be in love with disorder. Insecurity had seemed painful; someday I would be elated to feel so insecure. I would not need centeredness, stability, certainty; instead, I would crave the untidy, manifold richness of the world, which seemed even more miraculous, even more of a gift, than it had in the morning.

As I rode my Stingray back home, I still clung to the need for absolutes, but I could feel myself pedaling away from all that, toward a life in which ambiguity contributed to wonder. I would begin to let the ambiguities be themselves. Let people be very different from me, show me as much of their lives as I could stand. I was curious about their lives (as I pedaled home); boy, was I curious. How do they *do* that? (I looked around at the bedroom lights of Orange.) Strange as it sounds, I felt a sky-wide empathy for people, an admiration mixed with pity, revulsion, and amazement.

Contradiction and paradox give life its flavor: I could feel a day coming when I no longer believed in happiness as some static, unchanging state. It wasn't life I wanted, but living, a dynamic process full of whatever sadnesses and joys would be. I wasn't there yet, but I was pedaling there.

No, I don't "owe it all" to poetry; many of these changes would have happened anyway. I had, however, connected with years of humanity exploring its furthest reaches. I knew I had adopted a terribly complex insight, and that I would keep reading poetry to maintain and nourish it. Poetry has helped enlarge my powers of empathy and joy, my ability (as John Keats put it) to be in the midst of doubts and uncertainties without trying to solve them. I take more pleasure in people and in experience (car crashes, winning the lottery, writing a book, having children and gray hairs) than I otherwise would have. Why? Because I pay more attention now. That means there is more of life for me to experience, enjoy, and (let's face it) suffer than there would have been had I never read poetry. Not to be sentimental: my life is still mine, complete with responsibilities and problems. Whatever it is my future life will do to me, I know I will be there for it, more fully there, more alive to my own life.

I hope the same thing happens to you. Wait until it does—you'll know, DR. I wish you years of doing it.

## Appendix:

# Wordſ you might hear other people uſe when they talk about poetry

### Or A Glossary Of Poetic Terms

**P**oetry is for everyone. I'd rather people spoke about it the way they speak about most things—directly, from the heart, with a minimum of folderol. And most of the time, they do.

But, DR, poetry is a craft. It has its own professional language that speaks of things you find only in poems. Just as construction workers know about joists and drywall, just as mammalian cell biologists know about HPLC and gel electrophoresis, so readers and writers of poetry know about the special terms below. These terms can sometimes help us explain what we're seeing in a poem and help us appreciate the writer's skill.

I've arranged the terms under these headings:
☞ **Tools** (special things poets can do with language)
☞ **Music** (terms having to do with the sounds and rhythms of poetry)
☞ **Speaker, Situation, and Setting** (guess)
☞ **Forms** (different types of poems)
☞ **Traditions** (special topics about genres and history)

# Tools

**allusion**—a reference to something outside of the poem, such as people, places, events, or things in the present, the past, popular culture, or tradition. In C. P. Cavafy's poem "Ithaka" (page 72), you will find allusions to the Lestrygonians, Cyclops, and Poseidon. Poets make allusions to create **metaphors**, to bring new shades of meaning into a poem (think of the way Sylvia Plath uses references to Nazi history in "Daddy"), and to strike up a connection with the reader through shared knowledge.

**ambiguity**—the potential of possessing more than one meaning. Yes, DR, this word also means "obscurity" or "uncertainty." But poets deliberately cultivate the first kind of ambiguity, with marvelous effects. Often, they prefer that a poem's meaning remain unsettled—they want it to bristle with possibilities. Think of Helen Chasin's "The Word *Plum*" (page 13) or William Blake's "The Sick Rose" (page 97). Learn to play with ambiguity. See the very next entry.

**ambivalence**—a state of feeling that includes more than one emotion. (Ambivalence is often aroused by ambiguity.) Ambivalence (a good kind) is our natural state, DR. We feel happiness mixed with boredom, pleasure mixed with anxiety, resentment mixed with admiration. In other words, we rarely experience our emotions unalloyed. Good poetry (*like life, baby*) calls forth many combinations of feelings. Why demand an absolutely clear understanding, when it is so much richer to consider all the different things a poem *might* mean? You actually can destroy a good poem by demanding one single, certain meaning or emotion from it—so cultivate your capacity for ambivalence. It will help you as a reader and as a person, according to Lester Ganderfung of Telemarketing Center, New Jersey.

**apostrophe**—direct address to something or someone you wouldn't ordinarily address—as in Percy Bysshe Shelley's "O World, O Life, O Time."

**conceit**—a special kind of metaphor or simile in which the poet compares two things that are very dissimilar. See our excerpt from John Donne's "A Valediction: Forbidding Mourning" (page 106).

**diction**—a term generally used to mean "choice of words." The word *diction* also is used to mean groups of words with the same social register, as in *low diction* or *high diction*.

**enjambment**—the running of a sentence from one line into the next without punctuation. Remember "The Writer" by Richard Wilbur (page 6)?

> It is always a matter, my darling,
> Of life or death, as I had forgotten. I wish
> What I wished you before, but harder.

The way the second line runs into the third without a break is a good example of enjambment. Poets use this tool for all sorts of subtle effects. "I wish" hangs in the air for a moment—like wishing sometimes does. Then a surprise: "What I wished you before." Usually you wish for something new.

**figure of speech**—a word or group of words that are not to be taken literally but nevertheless express something recognizable—a very general classification that include metaphors, allusions, similes, and so forth

**image**—This word can mean

   ☞ a vivid picture

   ☞ a vivid appeal to any of the senses (not just vision)

   ☞ an instantaneous complex of emotions, often linked to a vivid picture or sense appeal (for a good example, see "Heat" by H.D., page 115)

   ☞ any **figure of speech**, including metaphors, personifications, similes, or allusions.

**inversion**—the practice, seen most often in poetry of older periods, of twisting words out of their natural order (see page 82)

**irony**—saying one thing when you mean something else. (Usually, the reader or hearer has clues as to what you really mean—otherwise, the irony wouldn't work.) There are many kinds of irony. In a common kind, you say the reverse of what you mean. Let's say I drop a dozen eggs on the floor. Your comment: "Well, *that* was smart." You were being ironic. In fact, you were indulging in **sarcasm**, a biting, sometimes hurtful form of irony.

Most irony is more subtle than sarcasm. In **understatement** the speaker says less than he or she means. If someone broadsides your car, smashing in the entire passenger's side, your comment might be, "Seems you put a little scratch on my door." One kind of understatement is **litotes**, in which the speaker makes a positive statement by negating that statement's opposite, as in "He is not underfed" instead of . . . well, let's be kind. In **overstatement** (also called **bathos**), the speaker says more than he or she means—exaggeration for the sake of effect. (For example, when you say to the Sunday driver who stove in your car, "You must be the best driver in the whole *world*!")

In **situational irony**, something happens at variance with your expectations—often directly contrary to those expectations—leaving a fatal or uneasy feeling. If a carton containing a hundred copies of this book fell out of a window and crushed me as I walked below, you'd say, "How ironic." John Gay's poem "My Own Epitaph" (page 43) is situationally ironic.

**metaphor**—an unspoken or implicit comparison between two things, implying identity. Poets do not use *like* or *as* in metaphors, and often they don't tell you a metaphor is happening at all. So how do you know? By being alert, especially when poets start speaking in ways you know aren't literally true. When they called Babe Ruth the Sultan of Swat, they weren't saying, "As you know, Babe Ruth is the ruler of the land of Swat." When George MacBeth writes "owl lives **/** by the claws of his brain," he is **not** saying that owls have a very strange brain anatomy. He is comparing (silently) the owl's instincts (the impulses in his brain) to claws. In "Ithaka" by C. P. Cavafy (see page 72), the poet compares the journey of life with a journey to the island of Ithaka. In "Getting Through," by Deborah Pope (see page 41), a communication breakdown is imagined as a telephone ringing in a long-abandoned house.

In its intensity, its psychological magic, metaphor is one of the poet's most important tools. When we think of one thing in terms of another—when we think of thing A as *being* thing B—new possibilities and points of view open up. Every day, probably every moment you speak, you use metaphors. I heard the following metaphors on the street over the past week:

Who died and made *you* king?
My meeting yesterday was a *nightmare*.
Back to the old grind.
Come on, man—I'm *dying* over here!
She looks down on everyone else.
He's a hunk.
You're a stupid pig, you know that?

I admit I am stupid, but I'm not really a pig. The person who called me a pig was using a metaphor comparing my stupidity with that of a particular animal. (Pigs, by the way, can be quite intelligent.) Metaphors are powerful *precisely because* they are unspoken. They call on us to imagine for ourselves all the ways in which, for example, a stupid person could resemble a pig, a well-built man might be a hunk of something, or an owl's instincts could be like claws.

Metaphors usually have two parts: the **tenor** (the thing being compared) and the **vehicle** (the thing the tenor is being compared to):

| tenor | vehicle |
|---|---|
| me | stupid pig |
| well-built man | hunk |
| life | journey to Ithaka |

If a metaphor extends all or much of the way through a poem, as it does in "Ithaka," we call it—drum roll—an **extended metaphor!** Cymbal crash!

**metonymy**—the practice of replacing the real name of a thing with the name of something associated with it. When we refer to the president as "the White House"or the king as "the crown," we are using metonymy.

**onomatopoeia**—a long word that appears in most glossaries of poetic terms. Seriously, onomatopoeia is the naming of a thing or action by imitating a sound associated with that thing. Onomatopoeic words include *moo, slosh, whizz, honk,* and *sproing.*

**oxymoron**—a statement that combines opposites. (Senate Intelligence Committee, as the joke goes.) Oxymoron is really a kind of irony, DR, because it shows how opposites can unexpectedly create uneasy realities. Read the following aloud, and ask yourself whether you have ever observed any of them in real life:

aggressive modesty
blockheaded genius
stingy generosity
victorious defeat

**personification**—the attribution of human qualities to nonhuman things

**simile**—a comparison between two things explicitly using the words *like* or *as*. For some beautiful similes, reread Adrienne Rich's "Song" (page 60) or Deborah Pope's "Getting Through" (page 41). Compare simile with **metaphor**.

**symbol**—something that stands for or suggests something else by association, resemblance, tradition, or relationship

**synecdoche**—not a town in mid-New York State, but the practice of naming a thing by substituting a part of that thing for the whole. Many nicknames are synecdoches. My wife calls me Bones. A mob boss might call his head bruiser Knuckles.

# Music

**Music** is a general term for the totality of a poem's sounds—including the rhythms, speed of lines, rhymes, vowels, consonants, and the combination(s) of any or all of these elements.

**accent**—see **stress**

**alliteration**—a term that most often means the repetition of consonant sounds. More generally, it also can mean the repetition of the same sounds in a group of neighboring words.

**assonance**—a term that most often means the repetition of vowel sounds. It can also mean the use of similar sounds in neighboring words or syllables.

**caesura**—the heaviest pause in the middle of a line of verse

**consonance**—harmonious or pleasing combinations of words or sounds; a great example is Tennyson's "Now Sleeps the Crimson Petal" (pages 27 and 142). Poets often use consonance to evoke comfortable, sensuous feelings in the reader.

**dissonance**—unharmonious combinations of sounds; poets often use dissonance to evoke discomfort in the reader. (Note: dissonance isn't always ugly. It can be very concrete, very beautiful.) See our excerpt from Seamus Heaney's "Death of a Naturalist" (page 29).

**foot**—a single rhythmical unit. The four most common feet are

| name | rhythm | example |
|------|--------|---------|
| iamb (iambic) | duh DAH | inDEED |
| trochee (trochaic) | DAH duh | THOUGHTless |
| anapest (anapestic) | duh duh DAH | in a TREE |
| dactyl (dactylic) | DAH duh duh | SPECimen |

The Greeks made up the names. The traditional way to make up a line of English poetry is to string together two or more of the same kind of foot. And what is a line?

**line**—a row of words, considered as a unit. In **free verse**, lines can be (and have to be) any length, any rhythm. But as I just mentioned, in more traditional poetry (free verse in English has a tradition of only 150 years), you build a line by stringing feet together. Regular repetition of a single foot or pattern of feet is known as **meter**.

Remember our discussion of the words *iambic pentameter* (page 23)? Iambic pentameter lines contain five **iambs**—and the resulting line is perhaps the most common (and, some people think, the most natural) kind of line in English. Many poets build lines by repeating the same kind of foot. Here are the names for repetitions of different frequencies:

monometer (one foot)
dimeter (two)
trimeter (three)
tetrameter (four)
pentameter (five)
hexameter (six)

and you can repeat and mix any of the feet we listed above.

**line speed**—the rapidity and ease with which you can read a line of poetry. You can read some lines quickly.

Shall I compare thee to a summer's day?

There's a lightness to the meaning and a corresponding swiftness to the line. But poets can also slow you down. Recall this line?

Death's second self, that seals up all in rest.

We slow down in the second example because it is clotted with heavy pauses at the ends of words, preventing you from passing lightly to the next word. Poets use line speed to reinforce the meaning of lines.

**meter**—a regular rhythmic pattern. Poets use meter to organize lines of poetry. See above, and also see our discussion of rhythm versus meter (pages 19–24). How can you tell if a poem has meter or not? Read a few lines. Note the stressed and unstressed syllables. If you find a pattern (or something close to one), your poem has meter. This practice is called **scansion**, by the way—scanning a poem's rhythmic pattern to determine the meter.

**rhetoric**—the total of all the words and turns of speech that make a poem persuasive or convincing

**rhyme**—repetition of sounds. Poets today are using rhyme in more ways than ever before. You have to stretch your understanding of rhyme, though. These ways include

**end rhyme**—repetition of sounds at the ends of lines, as in William Blake's poem "The Ecchoing Green":

The Sun does arise,
And make happy the skies.
The merry bells ring
To welcome the Spring.

This is the most familiar kind of rhyme, especially when it is

**exact rhyme**—repetition of precisely the same sound, as in *arise/skies* and *ring/Spring.*

**internal rhyme**—repetition of a sound within a line or across lines (anywhere but at the ends of lines). A tremendous example is our excerpt from Dylan Thomas's "And Death Shall Have No Dominion" (pages 25–26).

**sight rhyme**—the repetition of letters in words that do not rhyme by sound: *pain/again; gone/tone; whale/chorale.* Such pairs of words look as though they rhyme by sound, but they don't.

**slant rhyme**—inexact repetition of sounds. Slant rhyme is probably the most commonly used rhyme today. But poets have used it forever. Here is William Blake again, from "The Chimney Sweeper."

And so Tom awoke and we rose in the dark
And got with our bags & our brushes to work.

(In Blake's time *dark* and *work* probably were closer to exact rhyme—but they are slant rhyme now.) And remember "My Papa's Waltz" by our friend Theodore Roethke?

The whiskey on your breath
Could make a small boy dizzy;
But I hung on like death:
Such waltzing was not easy.

*Easy* is a lovely slant rhyme with *dizzy*. It's graceful, funny—and dizzy.

**vowel rhyme**—repetition of only the vowel sound in one or more words, as in *only/phone*; *breeze/machine*; *school/troops*. It's not exact rhyme, but it's rhyme. Remember "Two Girls" by Howard Nemerov (page 23)? Stretch those ears!

**rhythm**—the natural flow of stressed and unstressed syllables in poetry. Not the same as **meter**, which is a regular, superimposed pattern (see pages 19–24). People also speak of **visual rhythm** to describe the way a poem's lines look on the page.

**stress** (or **accent**)—the natural emphasis we place on syllables in a word. In the word *toMAto*, the syllable in the middle is stressed, and the other two are not. The way poets manipulate stress gives us the **rhythm** of **lines**.

# Situation, Speaker, and Setting

**character**—a fictional representation of an imaginary person

**occasion**—the special event, reason, condition, or cause that moves a poet to write a poem. See **occasional** poetry (page 168).

**persona**—the mask or character adopted by the poet. Pretty much the same as **speaker**, although the word *persona* sometimes is used to mean a speaker with an especially pronounced or complex personality, **situation**, or mental state.

**pose**—an attitude or role assumed for the sake of effect

**setting**—the time and place in which the events of a poem (or the speaker's rendition of those events) take place

**situation**—the state of affairs, conditions, or circumstances in which a poem takes place, or in which the speaker finds him- or herself

**speaker**—For the sake of discussion, we imagine a poem as being a *spoken* thing. So every poem has a speaker, a fictional character (created by the poet) who is speaking the poem. Poets, of course, do speak for themselves in many poems. In some instances, such as "On My First Son" by Ben Jonson (page 119), the poet clearly wants us to think that he himself is the speaker. But *don't* assume that the poet and the speaker are the same person unless the evidence for that connection is pretty heavy. Rather, assume that the poet has created a separate character to do the speaking.

Some poets will create a traditional or historical character through which to speak. (Robert Browning was a great one for that.) Others will strike an attitude—a **pose**—just to explore that attitude. Again, be careful. The poet may not agree with that attitude; he or she simply may want to see what it is like, satirize it, or dramatize it.

How can you tell whether speaker and poet are the same? And if they are not the same, how can you tell whether or not the poet agrees with the speaker? The answer, as usual: pay close attention. Sometimes you can tell and sometimes the best you can do is guess. But it's always worthwhile to look into the matter.

**tone**—the attitude of either the speaker or the poet. Usually, tone is attitude toward the subject matter of the poem. (Is the poet or speaker respectful? satirical? bored? hostile?) Much less often the word *tone* is used to mean attitude toward the audience.

**voice**—a word that can mean
☞ the personality of the speaker or poet
☞ the distinctive aspects of a poet's style
☞ **persona**

# Forms

**ballad**—Originally, ballads were folk poetry, written in short, musical, rhyming stanzas. Often they told sad, tragic, sometimes gory stories. People still write ballads all the time. Love poems, popular songs, and story poems often take the ballad form.

**blank verse**—unrhymed iambic pentameter. *Not* the same as **free verse**, which has no meter.

**concrete poetry**—verse that takes the shape of its subject. See May Swenson's "Night Practice" (page 66).

**confessional poetry**—a direct and truthful kind of verse, seemingly about the facts of the poet's life. Confessional poetry seems to tell us secrets, shocking material from which we normally turn away. This kind of poetry has always existed, but with poets in the 1950s and 1960s such as Robert Lowell, Sylvia Plath, and W. D. Snodgrass, confessional poetry became a kind of movement. Confessional poetry challenges us to remember the difference between the poet and the speaker, even when we're seemingly being told "this really happened *to me*."

**couplet**—a pair of lines that seem to belong together, often because of rhyme or stanza form

**dramatic monologue** (also called **soliloquy**)—a poem spoken by a single speaker, imagined as alone and speaking to him- or herself, exploring his or her situation or point of view

**epigram**—a very pointed poem, often very short. Here is one from a friend of mine:

> Here lies a woman, Mrs., Miss, or Ms—
> Now it doesn't matter which it is.

Epigrams are not always funny, but good ones always *tell*.

**epitaph**—a kind of **epigram** memorializing a deceased person

**free verse**—poetry that avoids regular meter and rhyme schemes

**ghazal**—an adaptation of an Arabic verse form. A ghazal is a series of couplets; the couplets may rhyme, or they may simply repeat a phrase in the second line of each couplet.

**haiku**—a Japanese poetic form. In English, haiku are **syllabic**, usually arranged in three lines, with syllables numbering 5-7-5. Here is one by Neja M. Hipto:

> moon and morning star
>     in autumn: man and woman
> dancing in a room

**performance poetry**—verse intended for public performance. Good performance poetry has all the virtues of good presentation—immediacy, emotional impact, power.

**prose poem**—a form that presents poetic language in unlined form

**soliloquy**—see **dramatic monologue**

**sonnet**—a poem in fourteen lines. Really, that's about it. Sonnets can be of almost any line length, rhymed or unrhymed. See our examples by Robert Frost (pages 38, 69–70), Howard Nemerov (page 23), and William Shakespeare (page 64).

**stanza**—a group of lines that appear to belong together. In traditional, rhymed poetry, each stanza takes the same form. In **free verse**, a stanza may be of any form or length.

**syllabic poetry**—verse written according to syllable count. In one kind of syllabic poem, each line contains the same number of syllables, as in this example from "Considering the Snail" by Thom Gunn:

> The snail pushes through a green
> night, for the grass is heavy
> with water and meets over
> the bright path he makes, where rain
> has darkened the earth's dark. He
> moves in a wood of desire

Seven syllables per line. In another kind of syllabic poetry, the poet cooks up stanzas in which the lines all have different fixed syllable counts: 1/5/9/13/9/7 and so on. See the excerpt from Marianne Moore's "The Fish" (pages 124–125).

# Traditions

**allegory**—a poem (or other artwork) that expresses universal human truths via fictional characters and actions, all of which have symbolic meanings

**Anglo-Saxon**—see **Old English**

**canon**—an authoritative list of the best or most significant poems (or paintings, songs, or other kinds of art). Canons can help us understand the history of poetry and can help us form our own ideas of what's good. But they have been abused. Don't let canons push you around. Like what you like.

**comedy**—a poem (or other artwork) that celebrates the persistence of humanity. Comedy has to do with people succeeding in some delightful way. Most comedy is funny, and most comedy ends well. One kind, **black comedy**, makes humor out of material we would ordinarily regard with dread.

**convention**—a general agreement about how to do something. Just as you find conventions in fashion (men's ties) or social behavior (handshakes), so you find poetic conventions. In **epic** poetry, or example, there is the convention of the **epic hero**'s descent into hell. In much love poetry, the loved one is described in conventional ways. A cliché (*cherry lips*—ugh—for example) is a convention that has died of overuse.

**didactic poetry**—verse that strongly advocates a point of view (e.g., **political poetry**) or aims to teach its audience (e.g., **moral poetry**)

**dramatic poetry**—verse that is meant (or is appropriate) for performance by actors

**elegy**—a poem of lamentation or sorrow

**epic**—a long public poem telling the story of how a community or nation came to be formed. A central figure called the **epic hero** faces the forces of nature, descends into hell, and risks life and limb in other **conventional** ways to bring the community into being.

**genre**—a type or kind of literature, poetry, or art: for example, **comic**, **epic**, or **tragic** poetry. Each genre brings into play a characteristic form or subject matter.

**light verse**—poetry that is playful or humorous. Light verse is usually rhymed. Sometimes people speak as if light verse were somehow "less important" than other kinds of poetry. Bunk.

**lyric poetry**—a catch-all term for short (usually), personal (usually), musical poetry. Lyric poetry normally is contrasted with **epic** poetry (which is communal in nature) and **dramatic** poetry (which is, well, dramatic). When most people think of poetry, they think of lyric poetry.

**myth**—a story that examines or explains the universe, a culture, or persistent and profound human questions or truths. Some well-known examples are the myths of Icarus and Daedelus, Paul Bunyan, and Superman.

**narrative poetry**—verse that tells a story

**occasional poetry**—poems written for specific occasions, such as births, deaths, marriages, battles, and invitations to supper

**Old English**—the earliest recorded version of English, spoken from before the 500s to shortly after the 1000s. Also called **Anglo-Saxon**, this is the language of *Beowulf* and other fine poetry. Many of the short, concrete, gruff words in English—*stone, man, house, knife*—are from Old English.

After the French invaded England in 1066, English changed rapidly. Middle English was spoken between 1100 and about 1500, Early Modern English between 1500 and 1750, and after about 1750 or so, just plain Modern English.

**parody**—a poem (or other kind of art) that makes fun of another poem (or other kind of art). Remember "This Is Just to Say" by William Carlos Williams (page 43)? Kenneth Koch has a poem entitled "Variations on a Theme by William Carlos Williams." Reread the Williams poem, then this:

DO IT

> We laughed at the hollyhocks together
> and then I sprayed them with lye.
> Forgive me. I simply do not know what I am doing.

That's a parody, DR.

**periods**—For convenience, we imagine history as being divided into periods, within which writers and artists are supposed to have something in common. Yes, DR, this practice is a fiction of convenience. Chaucer would have been surprised to hear that he was *medieval*. We've created periods to help us understand history and how poetry fits in. Here are some of the major periods of English and world literature, along with the length of time they cover. (These are my wildly approximate guesses, because almost everybody disagrees.)

**Homeric**—1000 B.C. to about 750 B.C.
**Classical**—750 B.C. to A.D. 476
**Dark Ages**—476-1000
**Medieval**—1000-1450
**Renaissance**—1450-1660
**Enlightenment**—1660-1798
**Romantic**—1798-1832
**Victorian**—1832-1901
**Edwardian**—1901-1910
**Modern**—1910-1945
**Postmodern**—1945 - present

And there are subdivisions and sub-subdivisions.

**satire**—a poem (or other kind of artwork) that holds up a particular social behavior for ridicule for the purpose of amendment

**tragedy**—a poem (or other artwork) that explores human limits by recounting the downfall of an admirable but flawed figure (the **tragic hero**). Tragedy explores how character is fate and vice versa.

**verse**—another word for *poetry*. Sometimes the word *verse* is used to distinguish metered, rhymed poetry from other kinds. The word *verse* may also mean

   ☞ a single **line** of poetry

   ☞ a single **stanza**

   ☞ **light verse**

Verse, DR, is what it could be.

# ACKNOWLEDGMENTS

"The City Limits" by A.R. Ammons from *A.R. Ammons: The Expanded Edition.* Copyright © 1986 by A.R. Ammons, reprinted by permission of W. W. Norton.

"In Memory of W.B. Yeats" and "Lullaby" from *W. H. Auden: Collected Poems* Copyrights © 1940 and renewed 1968 by W. H. Auden. Reprinted by permission of Random House, Inc.

"In Memory of Radio" from *The Le Roi Jones=Amiri Baraka Reader.* Copyright © 1991 by Amiri Baraka. Used by permission of the publisher, Thunder's Mouth Press.

Excerpts from "One Art," "The Fish," and "The Moose" from *The Complete Poems 1927-1979* by Elizabeth Bishop. Copyright © 1979, 1983 by Alice Helen Methfessel. Reprinted by permission of Farrar, Straus & Giroux, Inc.

"Coyote Wind" by Imogene Bolls reprinted by permission of *The Antioch Review.*

"The Word *Plum*", from *Coming Close and other Poems*, by Helen Chasin, reprinted by permission of Yale University Press.

"there is a girl inside" by Lucille Clifton Reprinted by permission of Curtis Brown Ltd., Copyright © 1980 by the University of Massachusetts Press. First Appeared in *two-headed woman* published by The University of Massachusetts Press.

"buffalo bill's"and "nine birds (rising" are reprinted from *Complete Poems: 1904-1962* by e.e. cummings, edited by George J. Firmage, by permission of Liveright Publishing Corporation. Copyright © 1923, 1950, 1951, 1978, 1991 by the Trustees for the e.e. cummings trust. Copyright © 1976, 1979 by George James Firmage.

Emily Dickinson's Poem #754 reprinted by permission of the publishers and the Trustees of Amherst College from *The Poems of Emily Dickinson*, Thomas H. Johnson, ed., Cambridge, Mass.: The Belknap Press of Harvard University Press, Copyright © 1951, 1955, 1979, 1983 by the President and Fellows of Harvard College.

"Gunslinger," from *Gunslinger* by Ed Dorn. Copyright © Duke University Press, 1989. Reprinted with permission.

Excerpts from "The Love Song of J. Alfred Prufrock" by T.S. Eliot reprinted by permission of Harcourt Brace Jovanovitch.

"Never Again Would Birds Song Be the Same," "Dust of Snow," and "The Silken Tent" from *The Poetry of Robert Frost* edited by Edward Connery Lathem. Copyright 1942, 1951 by Robert Frost. Copyright © 1970 by Lesley Frost Ballantine. Copyright 1923 © 1969 by Henry Holt and Co. Inc. Reprinted by permission of Henry Holt and Co., Inc.

"A Theory of Wind" by Albert Goldbarth reprinted by permission of Ontario Review Press.

"Heat" from *H.D.: Collected Poems, 1912-1944*. Copyright © 1982 by the estate of Hilda Doolittle. Reprinted by permission of New Directions Publishing Corp.

Excerpt from "Death of a Naturalist" from Selected Poems 1966-1987 by Seamus Heaney. Copyright © 1990 by Seamus Heaney. Reprinted by permission of Farrar, Straus & Giroux, Inc.

"Butcher's Son" by Joe Heithaus reprinted by permission of *The Antioch Review.*

Excerpt from "Morning After" from *Collected Poems* by Langston Hughes Copyright © 1994 by the Estate of Langston Hughes. Reprinted by permission of Alfred A Knopf, Inc.

**171**

# index

## a

accent *See* stress
Ackerman, Diane, 150
"Acquainted with the Night"
    (Frost), 111
advice in poetry, 70-73
The *Aeneid* (Vergil), 143, 144
aging in poetry, 63-66
Akhmatova, Anna, 90, 97, 135
*The Alchemist* (Jonson), 119
"All You Who Sleep Tonight"
    (Seth), 59, 64
*All You Who Sleep Tonight*
    (Seth), 140
allegory, 166
alliteration, 26, 160
allusion, 155
ambiguity, 64, 153-154, 156
ambivalence, 64, 153-154, 156
American culture and poetry, 4-
    8
Ammons, A. R., 91, 113, 121,
    146, 148
"Among School Children"
    (Yeats), 9
anapest, 160
"And Death Shall Have No
    Dominion" (Thomas), 25-26,
    162
Angelou, Maya, 3, 6
Anglo-Saxon, 166, 168
anthologies, 9, 86-88
"anyone lived in a pretty how
    town" (cummings), 103
apostrophe, 156
*Ariel* (Plath), 132
Armour, Richard, 141
art and poetry, 54-59

*The Art of Love* (Ovid), 129
*Ash Wednesday* (Eliot), 109
*Asphodel, That Greeny Flower*
    (Williams), 146, 147
assonance, 26
"At the Office Early" (Kooser),
    122
"At the San Francisco Airport"
    (Winters), 61-62, 64
atheism in poetry, 67-69
*An Atlas of the Difficult World*
    (Rich), 136
attention in poetry, 1, 10, 13, 30,
    37, 40, 42, and passim
Auden, W. H., 91-92, 97, 98, 106,
    110, 133, 137, 138, 141, 149
"Autres Bêtes, Autres Moeurs"
    (Nash), 126

## b

ballad, 164
Baraka, Amiri Imamu, 92-93,
    118
Bashō [Matsuo Munefusa], 93-
    94
bathos, 157
"Batter my heart, three-personed
    God; for you" [Holy Sonnet 17]
    (Donne), 106
beats, in reading poetry aloud,
    15-16, 18, 20
The Beatles, 7
Baudelaire, Charles, 94-95, 145
"The Bee Meeting" (Plath), 132
Beethoven, Ludwig van, 98, 99
Belitt, Ben, 91, 150
benefits of poetry, 9-10, 30, 77-
    78, 153-154, 168
*Beowulf*, 117, 144, 168
Berrigan, Ted, 103

Ono no, Komachi, 33
"On the Morning of Christ's
Nativity" (Milton), 123
"On the Pulse of Morning"
(Angelou), 3, 6
"One Art" (Bishop), 95
"One Train May Hide Another"
(Koch), 121
onomatopoeia, 159
oral pleasure in poetry, 29, 37,
40
ordinary language in poetry, 56-
58
Oresick, Peter, 7, 8
Ostriker, Alicia, 128-129, 133
other people's lives in poetry, 1,
9, 30, 52-74
overstatement, 157
Ovid [Publius Ovidius Naso], 89,
100, 129-130, 138
Owen, Wilfred, 90, 120, 130-
131
oxymoron, 159

## p

pace
in poetry *See* line speed
in reading poetry aloud, 16-17
*Paradise Lost* (Milton), 82, 123,
124
*Paradise Regained* (Milton), 123,
124
Parini, Jay, 150
parody, 168
Parra, Nicanor, 128
parting in poetry, 61-62
Pastan, Linda, 150
*Paterson* (Williams), 147
pauses
in poetry, 13, 15-17, 160

in reading poetry aloud, 13,
15-17
Paz, Octavio, 104, 128, 131-132
Peacock, Molly, 150
pentameter, 161
periods, 168-169
persona, 163, 164
performance poetry, 4-5, 48, 166
personification, 159
Petrarch, 100, 104
Petrosky, Anthony, 5
Pinsky, Robert, 113, 116, 127,
136, 146, 150
"Planetarium" (Rich), 136
Plath, Sylvia, 105, 115, 132-
133, 137, 138, 141, 155, 165
pleasure in poetry, 9, 37, passim
Poe, Edgar Allan, 94, 95, 133-134
poetry
advice in, 70-73
of aging, 63-66
American culture and, 4-8
appreciation of, passim
and art, 58-59
of atheism, 67-69
attention in, 1, 10, 13, 30, 37,
40, passim
benefits of, 9-10, 30, 77-78,
153-154
comfort in, 58-73
cost of, 48-49, 88
of death, 69-70
difficulty of, 7-8
in education, 3, 5-6, 8
emotional power of, 1, 62,
153-154
empathy and, 10, 32,
73-74, 154
emphasis in, 14-24
enunciation of, 14-17, 40
experience and, 1, 52-74
exploration in, 30, 35

# q r

pace of, 16-17
pauses in, 13, 15-17
sing-songyness in, 18
surprises in, 14-17
white spaces in, 15
"Rebirth of Slick" (Digable
Planets), 5
readings *See* performance poetry
religious belief and poetry, 52,
67-69
Renaissance period, 169
restraint in poetry, 61-62
Revell, Donald, 5, 9
rhetoric, 162
rhyme, 8, 14, 18-19, 25-26, 162-
163
rhythm
in poetry, 19-24, 65, 160-161,
163
in reading poetry aloud, 19-
24, 65, 159-166
Rich, Adrienne, 48, 60, 64, 89,
96, 105, 129, 133, 136-137,
138, 139, 159-160
Riding, Laura, 110
Ridler, Anne, 110
Rilke, Rainer Maria, 95, 104
Rimbaud, Arthur, 90, 95, 144, 145
"The Rime of the Ancient
Mariner" (Coleridge), 102
Ríos, Alberto, 150
"The Road Not Taken" (Frost),
110
Robinson, Edward Arlington, 98,
111, 152
Rochester, John Wilmot, Second
Earl of, 130
Roethke, Theodore, 18, 37, 96,
100, 114, 122, 130, 133, 137-
138, 162-163
Rogers, Pattiann, 91, 138, 146,
148

Romantic period, 169
"The Rose" (Williams), 147
Rosenberg, Isaac, 131
Rossetti, Christina, 134, 142
"Root Cellar" (Roethke), 37-38
Rukeyser, Muriel, 92, 96, 129,
138, 152

# S

"Sailing to Byzantium" (Yeats),
63
*Samson Agonistes* (Milton), 124
Sandburg, Carl, 118, 121, 146
Santos, Sherod, 150
Sappho, 90, 100, 138, 139
sarcasm, 157
Sarton, May, 105, 123, 138
Sassoon, Siegfried, 27, 131
satire, 169
scansion, 162
Schiller, Friedrich von, 97, 99
science and poetry, 52
Schnackenberg, Gjertrud, 116
Seetch, Beth, 150
"September 1913" (Yeats), 149
Seth, Vikram, 8, 10, 59, 64, 94,
95, 136, 139-140
setting, 43-47, 163-164
sex in poetry, 63-64, 129-130
Sexton, Anne, 105, 123, 129,
133, 137, 138
Shakespeare, William, 4, 48, 56,
64-65, 75-80, 106, 110, 118,
119, 140-141, 166
"Shall I compare thee to a
summer's day?" [Sonnet 18]
(Shakespeare), 161
Shange, Ntozake, 93, 118
Shapiro, Alan, 150
Shapiro, Karl, 114, 127

# U

# V

Vergil (Publius Vergilius Maro), 77, 84, 112, 117, 124, 129, 143-144

Verlaine, Paul, 90, 95, 144-145

verse, 169

Victorian period, 169

visual rhythm, 124-125, 163

*La Vita Nuova* (Dante), 104

vocabulary
in older poetry, 81-82
in poetry in general, 10

voice, 164

*Voices in the Family,* 6

*Volpone, or the Fox* (Jonson), 119

vowel rhyme, 25, 163

Wagoner, David, 150

Waldman, Anne, 150

*The Walls Do Not Fall* (H.D.), 115

*War Stories* (Nemerov), 127

*The Waste Land* (Eliot), 85, 107, 108, 109

Welles, Orson, 76

"West-Running Brook" (Frost), 110

"What a loss is here" (Bashō), 93

"What Work Is" (Levine), 54-55, 58

"When I Consider How My Light Is Spent" (Milton), 123

"When You Are Old" (Yeats), 149

white spaces *See also* line breaks, 15

Whitman, Walt, 4, 91, 93, 105, 111, 113, 121, 145-146, 147, 153

Wilbur, Richard, 6, 150, 156-157

Williams, C. K., 150

Williams, William Carlos, 43-44, 45, 93, 107, 115, 121, 125, 138, 146-147, 168

Winters, Yvor, 61, 64, 140

wisdom in poetry, 52-74

"The Word *Plum*" (Chasin), 12-16, 156

"The Wood-Pile" (Frost), 110

Wordsworth, William, 76, 97, 98, 99, 102, 120, 123, 126, 136, 138, 141, 147-148

working life in poetry, 54-58

Wright, Charles, 150

"The Writer" (Wilbur), 6, 106-107, 156-157

Wyatt, Sir Thomas (Thomas Wyatt the Elder), 81, 83, 141

Yeats, William Butler, 9, 63, 92, 97, 109, 110, 133, 137, 138, 141, 148-149

Yevtushenko, Yevgeny, 90

Young, Al, 4

## About the author

John Timpane is writer and lecturer at Lafayette College in Easton Pennsylvannia. He received his M.A. and Ph.D in English Literature from Stanford University. He is the recipient of the 1980 American Academy of Poets Prize and a 1984 Fulbright fellow.

## Write to us

BOAZ Publishing Company,
P.O. Box 6582, Albany, CA 94706,
and tell us what you like about poetry
and reading aloud.